Katharine Kuh

NEW YORK GRAPHIC SOCIETY ART LIBRARY

Break-up:
The Core of Modern Art

BREAK-UP: THE CORE OF MODERN ART

BOOKS BY **KATHARINE KUH**

Break-up: The Core of Modern Art

The Artist's Voice

Art Has Many Faces

Léger

Katharine Kuh

BREAK-UP

The core of modern art

New York Graphic
Society Ltd. Greenwich, Connecticut

First published in hardcover by New York Graphic Society Ltd., 1965.
Second printing, 1966.

Published as part of New York Graphic Society
Art Library Paperback Series, 1969.

Standard Book Number 8212-1107-2
Library of Congress Catalog Card Number 65-21745
Literary and reproduction rights reserved for all countries

Printed in Holland

TABLE OF CONTENTS

FOREWORD

This book does not purport to be a history of modern art, for it is more involved with content than data or dates. Deliberately condensed and always accompanied by visual evidence, the text examines works of art with only two objectives—to uncover meanings and motivations. Qualitative judgments are largely withheld as are also biographical details. The aim is to be as concise as possible.

The American artist, Mark Tobey, once astutely observed, "The content of a painting is tied up with time, place and history. It is always related to man's beliefs and disbeliefs, to his affirmations and negations. How we believe and disbelieve is mirrored in the art of our times." If one accepts this statement (and I do), then to understand art is to relate it to the life it comes from. Today certain basic symptoms, reflecting unrest and change, characterize the fine arts, literature, music, architecture, the dance and the theatre. An accelerated and sometimes syncopated tempo makes itself felt in every nerve center of our creative activity —in the cumulative repetitions of Gertrude Stein's words; in the modern film with its flashbacks and stream-of-consciousness interruptions; in the strident downbeat rhythms of jazz; in the contemporary dance, staccato and angular; in present-day architecture punctuated by its myriad reflecting glass windows. Not least revealing is the change that has occurred in personal handwriting, the flowing script of yesterday often replaced by illegible scratches. These are only a few familiar expressions that parallel the break-up we find in painting and sculpture. Why and how content, form, color, light, line, design and texture have been shattered during the last half century are questions investigated here in the hope that these findings may lead to a fuller understanding of modern art.

In describing the art of our times, certain adjectives reappear so frequently as to become virtual guideposts. Simultaneous, immediate, composite, transparent, multiple, condensed, fragmented, tangible, reconstructed—these are some of the key words. There are two others that are even more crucial: speed and space. This selected vocabulary has to do with many aspects of modern life, but particularly with our stepped-up rhythm and vastly extended visual horizons. Unexpectedly the world shrinks as it expands; there is a great deal more to see, and yet we see it faster. In trying to condense modern multiplicity into tangible form, artists have turned to certain shortcuts, to transparent, fragmented, reconstructed images where two compelling illusions—speed and space— act as basic source material.

I have always felt that books about art should be mainly visual and that words should be used chiefly to illuminate the experience of seeing. The language of literature can describe the language of vision, yet it can never stimulate the same emotions that original works of art arouse. Words can suggest a method of seeing but rarely induce us to see.

Though this volume is not intended as a picture book, the text through- out has been oriented to the works reproduced. These are seldom the only possible choices and are included more as representative examples and clues to further looking than as final selections. That reproductions, whether in color or black and white, are weak approximations of original works is doubly true when scale is drastically reduced. Illustrations are used here as practical guides to corroborate the text and to make even- tual encounters with original paintings and sculpture more enlightening.

I am very grateful to Harper & Row for allowing me to quote freely from my book *The Artist's Voice*, published in 1962. I am also indebted to the *Saturday Review* for certain excerpts from a number of articles I wrote for that magazine.

I have borrowed brief sections from my manual entitled *Looking at Modern Art* (1955) which was sponsored by the Fund for Adult Education and The Art Institute of Chicago.

K.K. *March 10, 1965 New York, New York*

BREAK-UP: THE CORE OF MODERN ART

CHAPTER 1

Break-up:
where, when and why

The art of our century has been characterized by shattered surfaces, broken color, segmented compositions, dissolving forms and shredded images. Curiously insistent is this consistent emphasis on break-up. However, dissolution today does not necessarily mean lack of discipline. It can also mean a new kind of discipline, for disintegration is often followed by reconstruction, the artist deliberately smashing his material only to reassemble it in new and unexpected relationships. Moreover, the process of breaking up is quite different from the process of breaking down. And during the last hundred years, every aspect of art has been broken up—color, light, pigment, form, line, content, space, surface and design.

In the nineteenth century, easels were moved out-of-doors and color was broken into relatively minute areas in order to approximate the reality of sunlight and to preserve on canvas nature's own fleeting atmospheric effects. Known as Impressionism, this movement was the first step in a long sequence of experiments that finally banished the Renaissance emphasis on humanism, on three-dimensional form and on a traditional center of interest. Here was the beginning of a gradual but steady tendency toward diffusion in art. A few years later, Vincent Van Gogh transformed broken color into broken pigment. Less interested in realistic light than in his own highly charged emotions, he allowed smashing rhythmic brushstrokes to mirror his personal turbulence. In doing so he foretold twentieth-century Expressionism, that aptly named movement which relied on pitted surfaces, broken outlines, unpredictable color and scarred textures to intensify emotional expression. As the Impressionists were bent on freeing nature from sham, so the Expressionists hoped to liberate their own feelings from all trace of artificiality.

Perhaps the most revolutionary break-up in modern art took place a little more than fifty years ago with the advent of Cubism. It was the Cubists, Picasso, Braque, Duchamp, Picabia, Léger, Delaunay and Juan Gris, who responded to the inordinate multiplicity of present-day life by breaking up and arbitrarily rearranging transparent planes and surfaces so that all sides of an object could be seen at once. As the Cubists broke through the boundaries of conventional form to show multiple aspects simultaneously, their Italian colleagues, the Futurists, hoped to encompass the uninterrupted motion of an object at one time. This they tried to do by a series of overlapping transparent forms illustrating the path of an object as it moved through space.

With Surrealism came still another kind of break-up, the break-up of chronology. Frankly influenced by Freudian discoveries, this movement splintered time sequence with an abandon borrowed from the world of fragmented dreams. Content was purposely unhinged in denial of all rational expression, allowing disconnected episodes to re-create the disturbing life of our unconscious. At the same time, perspective and distance often became severely dislocated. Denying the orderly naturalism of the Renaissance, painters today project space and distance from innumerable eye levels, intentionally segmenting their compositions into conflicting perspectives. We look from above, from below, from diverse angles, from near, from far—all at one and the same time (not an unfamiliar experience for eyes accustomed to air travel). Here again is the Cubist idea of simultaneity, the twentieth-century urge to approach a scene from many different directions in a single condensed encounter.

Finally we come to the total break-up of Abstract Expressionism, a technique that celebrates the specific act of painting (sometimes appropriately called Action Painting). Now everything is shattered—line, light, color, form, pigment, surface and design. These canvases defy all the old rules as they reveal the immediate spontaneous feelings of the artist in the process of painting. There is no one central idea, no beginning, no end—only an incessant flow and flux where lightning brushstrokes report the artist's impulsive and compulsive reactions. The pigment actually develops a life of its own, almost strong enough to hypnotize the painter. Here break-up turns into both content and form, with the impetuous paint itself telling the full story. No naturalistic image is needed to describe these artists' volatile feelings.

As one looks back over the last hundred years, the history of break-up becomes a key to the history of art. Why painters and sculptors of this period have been so involved with problems of dissolution is a question only partly answered by the obvious impact of modern scientific methods of destruction. One cannot deny that the last two devastating wars and the possibility of a still more devastating one to come do affect our daily thinking. Since the discovery of the atom bomb, science has become almost synonymous with destruction. The influence of contemporary warfare with its colossal explosions and upheavals has unquestionably had much to do with the tendency toward fragmentation in art, but there have been other and earlier causes.

From the beginning, it was science in one form or another that affected modern painting and sculpture. In nineteenth-century Europe the interest in atmospheric phenomena was not an isolated expression limited to the Impressionists. At that time, numerous scientists were experimenting with all manner of optical color laws, writing widely on the subject as they investigated the relationship of color to the human eye. Artists like Monet and Seurat were familiar with these findings and not unnaturally applied them to their paintings. It would be a grave mistake to underestimate the influence of contemporary scientific research on the development of Impressionism. The wonders of natural light became a focus for nineteenth-century artists exactly as the magic of artificial light stimulated painters of the present century. If the earlier men were more interested in rural landscapes seen out-of-doors in the sunlight, the later artists quite reasonably concentrated on city scenes, preferably at night when man-made luminosity tends to puncture both form and space.

Other scientific investigations also exerted considerable influence on present-day painters and sculptors. Inventions like the microscope and telescope, with their capacity to enlarge, isolate and probe, offer the artist provocative new worlds to explore. These instruments, which break up structures only to examine them more fully, demonstrate how details can be magnified and separated from the whole and operate as new experiences. Repeatedly artists in recent years have exploited this idea, allowing one isolated symbol to represent an entire complex organism. Miró often needs merely part of a woman's body to describe all women, or Léger, one magnified letter of the alphabet to conjure up the numberless printed words that daily bombard us.

As scientists smash the atom, so likewise artists smash traditional forms. For how, indeed, can anyone remain immune to the new mushroom shape that haunts us day and night? The American painter, Morris Graves, put it well recently, "You simply can't keep the world out any longer. Like everyone else, I've been caught in our scientific culture." This is not to say that painters are interested in reproducing realistic scenes of atomic explosions, but rather that they are concerned with the reactions accompanying these disasters. It is just possible that, with their extra-sensitized intuition, artists may have unconsciously predicted the discovery of atomic energy long before "the bomb" became a familiar household word, for the history of break-up in art antedates the history of nuclear break-up.

Even the invention of the X-ray machine has brought us closer to penetrating form. We no longer think of outer coverings as solid or final; we know they can be visually pierced merely by rendering them transparent. We have also learned from science that space penetrates everything.

The sculptor Gabo claims, "Space is a reality in all of our experiences and it is present in every object... That's what I've tried to show in certain of my stone carvings. When they turn, observe how their curved forms seem interpenetrated by space." For the artist today, nothing is static or permanent. The new popular dances are no more potently kinetic than the new staccato art forms that everywhere confront us.

With the dramatic development of speedier transportation and swifter communication comes a visual overlapping responsible for much of contemporary art. In modern life one is simultaneously subjected to countless experiences that become fragmented, superimposed, and finally rebuilt into new experiences. Speed is a cogent part of our daily life.

How natural, then, that artists reflect this pressure by showing all sides of an object, its entire motion, its total psychological content in one concerted impact. It is almost as if the pressures of time had necessitated a visual speed-up not unlike the industrial one associated with the assembly line and mass production. Speed with its multiple overlays transforms our surroundings into jagged, interrupted images.

Modern technology and science have produced a wealth of new materials and new ways of using old materials. For the artist this means wider opportunities. There is no doubt that the limitations of materials and nature of tools both restrict and shape a man's work. Observe how the development of plastics and light metals along with new methods of welding and brazing have changed the direction of sculpture. Transparent plastic materials allow one to look through an object, to see its various sides superimposed on each other (as in Cubism or in an X-ray). Today, welding is as prevalent as casting was in the past. This new method encourages open designs, often of great linear agility, where surrounding and intervening space becomes as important as form itself. In fact, it becomes a kind of negative form. While bronze casting and stone carving are techniques more readily adapted to solid volumes, welding permits perforated metal designs of extreme versatility that free sculpture from the static restrictions which for centuries have moored it to the floor.

More ambiguous than other scientific inventions familiar to modern artists, but no less influential, are the psychoanalytic studies of Freud and his followers, discoveries that have infiltrated recent art, especially Surrealism. The Surrealists, in their struggle to escape the monotony and frustrations of everyday life, claimed that dreams were the only hope. Turning to the irrational world of their unconscious, they banished all time barriers and moral judgments to combine disconnected dream experiences from the past, present and intervening psychological states. The Surrealists were concerned with overlapping emotions more than with overlapping forms. Their paintings often become segmented capsules of associative experiences. For them, obsessive and often unrelated images replaced the direct emotional messages of Expressionism. They did not need to smash pigment and texture; they went beyond this to smash the whole continuity of logical thought.

There is little doubt that contemporary art has taken much from contemporary life. In a period when science has made revolutionary strides, artists in their studios have not been unaware of scientists in their laboratories. But this has rarely been a one-way street. Painters and sculptors, though admittedly influenced by modern science, have also molded and changed our world. If break-up has been a vital part of their expression, it has not always been a symbol of destruction. Quite the contrary; it has been used to examine more fully, to penetrate more deeply, to analyze more thoroughly, to enlarge, isolate and make more familiar certain aspects of life that earlier we were apt to neglect. In addition, it sometimes provides rich multiple experiences so organized as not merely to reflect our world, but in fact to interpret it.

CHAPTER 2

Break-up of color

1. CLAUDE MONET, French, 1840–1926
TWO HAYSTACKS, 1891,

2. CLAUDE MONET, TWO HAYSTACKS, 1891

Claude Monet, definitive leader of French Impressionism, often painted nearly identical versions of the same scene, varying chiefly the time of day or time of year. In 1891 he exhibited no less than fifteen canvases all devoted to haystacks done at different hours and seasons. Obviously his interest was not the haystacks *per se*, though at times he invested these familiar forms with the poetry of Oriental pagodas. His concern was less with rural landscapes than with the way light, in its multiple aspects, changed these landscapes. And so he chose subjects that best absorb, refract and reflect light.

Haystacks with their bristling broken surfaces and pyramidal shapes were well adapted to his needs; so also were shimmering poplar trees, reflections in Venetian canals, scenes of London in mist and fog, and the façade of Rouen Cathedral, a late, lace-like Gothic structure. From these subjects came many of Monet's most successful series.

What he wanted was to reproduce the effects of realistic sunlight, a radical idea in the nineteenth century when the average artist was still firmly committed to conventional studio procedures. Traditional painters of the period found Monet, Sisley, Pissarro, Renoir and the other Impressionists slightly mad when these artists moved their easels out-of-doors and painted not only *in* the light but actually made light the sole *focus* of their paintings. Claiming that color is light and that when light changes, color changes, Monet felt that minute atmospheric transformations could best be recorded by relying on many different canvases, each painted at a different hour. It was only the landscape itself that remained

16

1

constant. Incidentally, this very indifference to subject matter paved the way for abstract art.

Monet contended that solely by means of broken color could changing luminosity be approximated. The Impressionists felt that this was nature's own way, that sunlight tends to break color into multiple facets. These men hoped literally to duplicate nature's methods. As far as light and color were concerned they were ardent realists, but since they sublimated everything to the demands of naturalistic luminosity, other aspects of their work, notably form, distance and composition, became more cursory. In both haystack canvases Monet applied color loosely in small patches, recording patiently every nuance of fluctuating light with such validity that one almost senses the precise hour each picture was painted.

3. CLAUDE MONET, CHARING CROSS BRIDGE, 1899–1904

As he grew older Monet tended to disperse color over the entire surface of his canvas, disregarding traditional form, depth, design and line even more than in his earlier years. His concern with the tidal ebb and flow of nature's forces turned his late paintings into pulsating near-abstractions where break-up of color was used less to depict light than to express his own emotions. Though we usually think of Monet as the father of Impressionism, in recent years we recognize him as far more than a student of luminosity. No one denies that light always remained his consuming interest, but his late work went beyond the facts of nature to encompass his own personal feelings in the presence of nature.

Like many other artists, he was attracted by the mists of London, which he invested with mysterious overtones. Using strips of divided color, he gave immediacy to his own spontaneous reactions. Now he observed his inner nature with the same urgency as earlier he had observed the outer world of nature. In the painting "Charing Cross Bridge," architecture, water and reflections are fused together in an hallucinated maze, making it impossible to separate shadow from substance. Monet's was a world of dense shimmering color where forms became lost in surface richness. Though, as the years passed, he continued to divide his color, he eventually shifted his objective. Moving gradually from Impressionism to Expressionism and virtually combining the two, he developed a way of seeing that was to have pronounced repercussions on recent abstract art.

4. GEORGES SEURAT, French, 1859–1891
SUNDAY AFTERNOON ON THE ISLAND OF LA GRANDE JATTE,
1884–1886

5. GEORGES SEURAT,
SUNDAY AFTERNOON ON THE ISLAND OF LA GRANDE JATTE, Detail

Georges Seurat also depended on broken color, but with such disciplined
severity as to result in the utmost restraint. "La Grande Jatte," usually
considered his masterpiece and surely one of the greatest paintings of the
nineteenth century, does far more than celebrate a charming bourgeois
scene. Designed with classical precision, this composition is an extraordinary study in horizontals and verticals, dark and light, form and
distance, line and volume. Each figure, each shadow, each tree has been
carefully related to the whole plan so that the eye moves across and back
into this large canvas with a leisurely sense of discovery. Here form, line
and depth do not melt in strong light as was true of Impressionism, for
Seurat wanted to go beyond the representation of sunlight; he wanted
to give his painting a feeling of unalterable permanency while yet making
it seem a source of light. To this end he employed a new technique, using

5

a complete palette of pure color and applying pigment in dots small enough to blend when seen at a distance—a method known as the optical mixture. Scientific discoveries of the nineteenth century, particularly those related to optical color laws, were undoubtedly responsible for Seurat's deep interest in the relationship of color to the human eye. He learned that complementary hues applied in small contrasting areas make for greater luminosity. Because his work evolved from Impressionism but pushed the study of light and color further, it is sometimes called Neo-Impressionism. The same patience he lavished on his tiny separated dots of color was also directed toward the structure of his paintings. Only after dozens of preliminary sketches did he finally combine his material into a major work like "La Grande Jatte."

6. **AUGUSTE RODIN,** French, 1840–1917
   MAN WITH THE BROKEN NOSE, 1864, Bronze

7. **MEDARDO ROSSO,** Italian, 1858–1928
   HEAD OF A YOUNG WOMAN, c. 1901, Wax over plaster

Two nineteenth-century artists transferred Impressionism to sculpture, forcing light to break up the surface of their forms very much as painters of the period allowed it to break up color. Certain pieces by Auguste

6

Rodin and Medardo Rosso exploit luminosity to such a degree that these works seem bathed in fluctuating tints of warm color rather than in the dark and light tones usually reserved for sculpture. Both men deliberately modelled their surfaces so that multiple irregularities attracted highlights and shadows. Repeatedly one feels the imprint of thumb and finger intentionally making hollows and ridges exaggerate contrasts of surface coloration. Rodin once said, "As paradoxical as it may seem, a great sculptor is as much a colorist as the best painter... Color is the flower of fine modelling."

These two men, who were familiar with each other's work, were after the same evanescent effects as painters of the period. When light ripples over their sculpture, one senses a fluidity that melts form and reveals palpitating movement beneath its surface.

Rosso, an important forerunner of Italian Futurism, predicted that dynamic movement with his strangely tilted volatile figures often modelled in fleeting wax, a medium he preferred because it offered him freedom in manipulating surface variations. When he and Rodin dematerialized form, they were frankly using painterly methods. For them, contrasts of light and dark playing over broken surfaces contributed to the dramatic expression they both were after.

CHAPTER 3

Break-up of pigment

8. VINCENT VAN GOGH, Dutch, 1853–1890
OLIVE TREES, 1889

While Van Gogh was living in Paris with his brother Theo, he became interested in French Impressionism; yet once he reached the south of France, his way of working and his way of seeing changed dramatically. The hot sun, the almost tropical vegetation, the strong hard light stimulated him as much as his loneliness and mounting despair tormented him. Far earlier than Monet, he envisioned nature as an instrument for revealing strong personal emotions. Instead of stressing densely interpenetrated broken areas of color, as Monet was to do in his late work, Van Gogh emphasized broken pigment. He used streaking brushstrokes heavy with paint to construct blazing canvases.

In the "Olive Trees" one finds form, line, distance, light, design—in short, everything—depending for definition on broken pigment applied in agitated strips. Van Gogh actually drew with his paint, making each stabbing brushstroke a testament to his magnificent draughtsmanship and to his tumultuous emotions. As Monet's haystacks turn into Oriental pagodas, so Van Gogh's trees metamorphose into licking flames. These riotous branches, tree trunks and leaves, this waving grass and streaked sky, all constantly in motion, tell us more about the artist himself, his anxieties and passions, than about any specific landscape. Nor could familiar or traditional methods have described his chaotic feelings with such direct authenticity.

Van Gogh's renunciation of academic techniques was not as deliberate as it may seem. Driven by his own needs, he took unconscious liberties with nature, turning his paintings into revealing autobiographical records. Curiously, his work always speaks of familiar human emotions

even when human beings do not appear. Because he came after Impressionism and evolved from it, he is labeled a Post-Impressionist, but in truth Van Gogh was the first completely modern Expressionist, an artist who sacrificed naturalistic appearances in a headlong search for himself.

9. CHAIM SOUTINE, Russian, 1894–1944
SQUARE IN A SMALL TOWN, VENCE, 1929

Chaim Soutine found in Van Gogh his guiding spirit. Both men, whose canvases from beginning to end were dedicated to passionate emotional expression, personalized nature, endowing trees with metaphysical overtones and branches with fiery gestures. Soutine's methods echoed Van

9

Gogh's; he too depended on writhing broken strips of pigment to describe landscapes, human figures and still lifes, but most particularly he used this technique to describe himself. Another man might view a village square in Vence as a routine experience. Not so Soutine, who turned it into a lurching scene, more closely related to his own agitation than to a quiet French plaza.

The use of loose broken pigment to express personal emotions is not new, but only during the present century has this method been exploited to its fullest. With Soutine, sometimes the paint becomes so tortured as to obliterate all semblance of subject. It is interesting to recall how many painters, as they matured, tended to free themselves from the tight restrictions of their youth. Artists like Titian, Rembrandt, Turner, Cézanne and Degas in their late years frankly avoided meticulous methods in favor of a more instinctual spontaneity.

10. GEORGES ROUAULT, French, 1871–1958
HEAD OF CHRIST, 1905

11. CHRIST, French, 12th century, Stone

During Rouault's long career he rarely surpassed the intensity of his early religious paintings. Even when he chose judges, prostitutes or clowns as modern subjects, his work seemed to stem consistently from medieval sources. At heart a moralist concerned with social problems, he used the shorthand methods of his own century, rapidly brushing in his figures with broken strokes of thick paint. "Head of Christ" recalls the aged and eroded stone Christs carved by anonymous craftsmen of the Middle Ages. Repeatedly, modern artists have turned for inspiration to this period, avoiding, as a rule, the more finished style of the Renaissance, which came to them watered down through academic nineteenth-century imitators. Consciously turning their backs on artificiality, and by the same token eliminating whatever they considered "prettified," shallow or overfastidious, artists like Rouault were products of a revolution aimed at nineteenth-century complacency. In their zeal for honest emotional expression they sometimes confused the legitimate accomplishments of Renaissance art with the sterility of its followers.

10   11

In "Head of Christ" it was not so much his own emotions that Rouault revealed; it was more those of a suffering mankind. Symbolically, the idea of pain takes over the entire painting, broken lines in the face no less cruelly stabbing than those in the crown of thorns.

12. OSKAR KOKOSCHKA, Austrian, 1886–
 PORTRAIT OF MAX REINHARDT, 1919, Lithograph

13. EDVARD MUNCH, Norwegian, 1863–1944
 THE CRY, 1895, Lithograph

In Germany between the two world wars a strongly emotional movement developed, so insistent that it came to be known as German Expressionism. Curiously, its two greatest leaders were not Germans. I refer to the Norwegian, Edvard Munch, and the Austrian, Oskar Kokoschka. Native German Expressionists differed from their European colleagues mainly in degree. The Germans tended toward greater brutality and more vitriolic anger, not surprising in artists whose medieval ancestors were specialists in savage realism.

Though we do not customarily connect pigment with lithographs, still these prints by Munch and Kokoschka were conceived in wide smashing lines more reminiscent of brush and paint than of graphic techniques. In Kokoschka's portrait, splintered contours perform double duty; they suggest the tense restlessness of the sitter (in this case, the famous theatre director, Max Reinhardt) and yet go further to show him almost in motion, his mobile face caught in a moment of changing thought. With urgent economy and staccato speed, Kokoschka reveals a complex personality. The nervous unfinished quality of the drawing contributes to the idea of immediacy, making us feel we are in the studio watching the artist as he works directly from his model. No likeness could be more intimate and revealing; none could be more opposed to that long portrait tradition associated with officialdom.

As Van Gogh and Soutine used broken pigment to underline their own emotions, Rouault and Kokoschka more often let it express the

12   13

emotions of their subjects, but always at a given moment and under specific circumstances. How Reinhardt looked is less important than how he felt.

As for "The Cry" by Munch, where in the entire history of art has the horror of frozen fear been better expressed? Like Van Gogh's streaks of pigment, Munch's heavy lines break his lithograph into an agitated, stylized landscape. Opposing ribbons of black do more than isolate a ghost-like face; they also set up restless tensions, inducing an almost unbearable suspense.

14. FRANCIS BACON, British, 1910–
STUDY AFTER VELASQUEZ' PORTRAIT OF POPE INNOCENT X, 1953

Though the British artist, Francis Bacon, had not seen Velasquez' portrait of Pope Innocent X when he painted this study, he was familiar with photographs of it and had already produced several canvases paraphrasing the painting. Much impressed by experimental modern films, especially those of the great Russian pioneer, Eisenstein, Bacon here built an image based on fluid cinematic techniques. His transparent figure ripples and moves, suggesting a hollow presence behind diaphanous robes. In "The Cry" by Munch (Plate 13) we sense a tangible sound—a shrill screech—but in Bacon's painting the horrifying open mouth recalls those frustrating dreams where we strain to scream and yet make no sound. The figure becomes strangely ambiguous; one can never be certain whether it is seated behind or before the curtain, whether it is entangled in the curtain, or only a projection on the curtain as, in fact, a film would be. Form is dematerialized both psychologically and physically. The figure moves and yet is frozen; the figure cries and yet is silent; the figure is caged and yet eludes its barriers by melting into the surrounding curtain, a curtain too dense to penetrate. Only the figure is vulnerable. In recent art, man seldom wins.

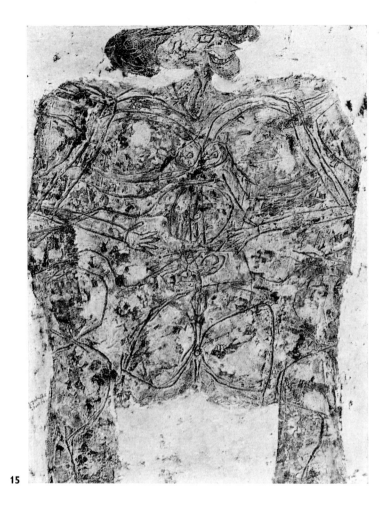

15

15. JEAN DUBUFFET, French, 1901–
LE METAFISYK (Corps de Dame), 1950

16. WAR PHOTOGRAPH

If Rouault bypassed the Renaissance to borrow from the Middle Ages, another Frenchman, Jean Dubuffet, skirted all accepted traditions to ally himself with the savage images of primitive man. Dubuffet once said, "Personally, I believe very much in values of savagery; I mean: instinct, passion, mood, violence, madness.... Painting is, in my opinion, a language more rich than that of words...a language more charged

with meaning.... Further, painting manipulates materials which are themselves living substances."

And here is the key to Dubuffet's art. With heavy pigment manipulated and kneaded in low relief, he exploits pitted surfaces in order to give urgency to emotional content. In many of his paintings, harried pigment suggests those eroding processes we associate with death. But paradoxically the pigment itself is always alive, moving, despite dense incrustations. While Van Gogh drew with strips of pigment, Dubuffet does the reverse, superimposing or incising occasional lines of definition on his richly decomposing paint. Here, the body of a woman recalls a scarred battlefield. If one compares photographic evidence from a war-torn city with a figure by Dubuffet, one realizes how strong a role disintegration plays in his work.

But it is not merely destruction that interests Dubuffet. No matter how tortured his subject, he endows it with life and feverish intensity. For him, the greatest sin is indifference. "Many people," he once said, "have imagined that I am predisposed to disparage, that I get pleasure from showing wretched things. What a misunderstanding! It was my intention to reveal to them that it is exactly those things they thought ugly, those things which they forgot to look at which are in fact very marvelous."

33

17. HYMAN BLOOM, American, 1913–
OLD WOMAN DREAMING, c. 1958, Gouache

The American artist Hyman Bloom allows a purposely harassed surface to intensify his nightmare scene. The bruised pigment of this gouache seems to parallel the veined, gnarled, wrinkled skin of the aged hag whose head almost dematerializes in the surrounding pillows. Looking down from above, we find the old woman's face contorted by terrifying dreams. Though she is alive, the hand of death is immanent, for this is a skeletal vision exaggerated by decomposing pigment.

One should not underestimate the strong hold despair, disgust and negation seem to exert on artists today. Few view the world with optimism. And this is not limited to painters and sculptors; writers, especially the Existentialists, are equally nihilistic. There is no easy explanation for the present pessimism, unless the wider understanding we now bring to our own unconscious reactions makes us at once more tolerant and more realistic. Perhaps present-day artists depict a shattered world precisely because they are able to face destruction and even find esthetic value in its waste. After all, in our century we have witnessed physical destruction on an unparalleled scale. For artists like Dubuffet and Bloom, break-up has literally become a new form. Rejecting all discreet codes and moral restrictions, they deal with vital forces, brutal, uncouth and disturbing, but vigorously alive. Ironically, the very death they describe gives life to their brushes.

18

19

18. **HENRI MATISSE,** French, 1869–1954
   THE SLAVE, 1900–1903, Bronze

19. **ALBERTO GIACOMETTI,** Swiss, 1901–1966
   PORTRAIT OF DIEGO, Bronze

20. **JEAN DUBUFFET,** French, 1901–
   THE JOVIAL ONE, 1959, Papier-mâché

20

These three figures exploit broken surfaces in order to stress emotional content. As painters exaggerate broken pigment, so sculptors depend on surface irregularities for the same purpose. Matisse and Giacometti indented their bronze figures with abrasions and crevices, reminding one constantly of the hands that molded the original clay. Though Giacometti's portrait bust of his brother was made a half century after Matisse's "Slave," and though it is more ruggedly modelled, both figures grow out of the same affirmation. These broken contours, where thumb and finger intentionally remove every vestige of academic polish, are symptomatic of the emphasis our times place on direct emotions. In each case, outer form is distorted in order to uncover inner feeling.

Even more direct is Dubuffet's papier-mâché head called "The Jovial One." The artist undoubtedly chose this malleable material because it lent itself readily to the furrowed surfaces he prefers. What better way to demonstrate that art does not rely on permanent, valuable trappings than to select an expendable material like paper? Pushing the same idea further, Dubuffet often creates clinker sculptures from burnt-up, cast-off cinders. For him, art is always expendable; he expects it to disintegrate no less than man.

The three figures reproduced here are all human characterizations, at once noble, ludicrous and awkward, but also uncompromising, personal and expressive. We are made aware of the artists' direct methods (there are no hidden studio techniques here), of how their means parallel their needs.

CHAPTER 4

Break-up of form

21. PAUL CÉZANNE, French, 1839–1906
MONT SAINTE-VICTOIRE, 1904–1906

In his late work Cézanne used transparent forms to expose basic inner structures. Earlier, he had followed the Impressionists' search for luminosity, but light was never his real interest. For him, it was form and distance that counted. His experiments in these fields were to have indelible impact on the art of our century. Observe how in his late landscape "Mont Sainte-Victoire," planes are simplified, broken up and reduced to transparent cubes, revealing the geometric structure of mountain, trees and houses. This is far more than an ordinary landscape; it is also more than a study of fragmented planes, for here Cézanne created an organized excursion in depth and space where objects in the fore and middle ground act as foils to be looked through and beyond. Each line, each form, each translucent plane contributes to the illusion of recession. Cézanne, who was not concerned with transient motions or emotions, devoted his life to the exploration of permanent values. Always in search of basic truths, he concentrated less on naturalistic appearances than on the *nature* of underlying form. When he painted a landscape it was not a specific scene he projected but a generic one common to all landscapes. Though he was a contemporary of Van Gogh, never were two men more dissimilar. Yet it is they who exerted the strongest influence on modern art—Van Gogh as the father of Expressionism and Cézanne as the forerunner of Cubism.

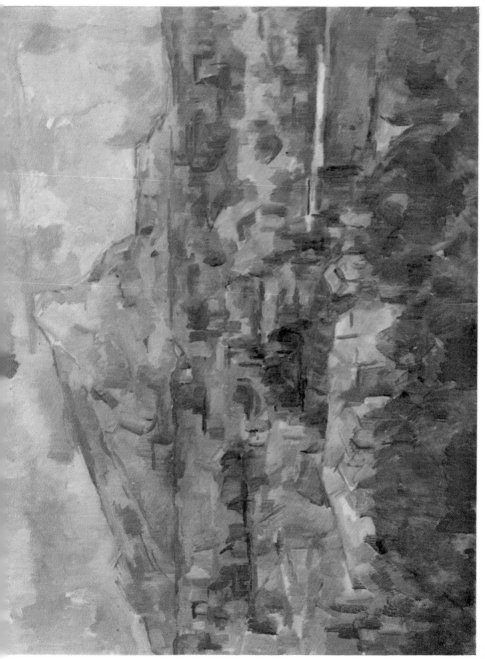

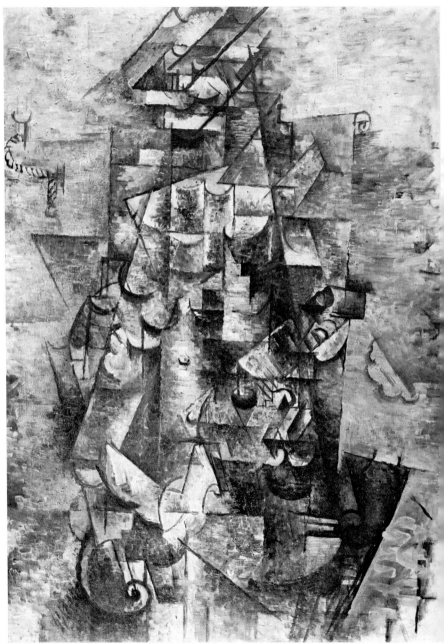

22. GEORGES BRAQUE, French, 1882–1963
MAN WITH A GUITAR, 1911

Unlike Expressionism, Cubism was not a continuation, a modification or even an intensification of earlier art movements. It was the beginning of a new idea, an idea which was to transform the twentieth century visually. As the most important art experiment of our period, Cubism influenced architecture, advertising, textiles and industrial design. This movement, which was basically concerned with the break-up and arbitrary rearrangement of form, was not without debt to Cézanne and Negro sculpture. Responding to the angular stylizations of African carvings and to the geometric experiments of Cézanne, such artists as Braque, Picasso and Juan Gris developed Cubism. But it was more than a method; it was a philosophy, a new way of thinking and seeing.

In "Man with a Guitar" Braque broke up forms into an almost non-recognizable design, his planes inverted, rearranged and superimposed on each other in shallow depth. Gone is the deep space of Cézanne; gone is all naturalistic perspective. What remained was a new freedom that permitted artists to decompose objects and then restructure them. In its simplest, most orthodox form, Cubism was an attempt to show all sides of an object at one time. It was an ambitious experiment concerned with recreating the multiplicity of modern life in visual terms. Depending on familiar daily objects as points of departure, the Cubists revitalized our way of seeing by showing us innumerable kaleidoscopic possibilities. As artists, they took the liberty of condensing many visual experiences into a final composition.

23. JEAN METZINGER, French, 1883–1956
WOMAN WITH FAN, 1913

Metzinger painted one of the first multiple-faced figures of the present century. "Woman with Fan" may possibly be the earliest version of a long series that includes innumerable examples of the same subject by Picasso and Braque. In Metzinger's canvas, the workings of Cubism are easily deciphered, for here one clearly sees how the artist superimposed different aspects of the same face on each other. The woman appears in profile, in front view and at various angles. Her fan is found both at the bottom and top of the composition, sometimes open, sometimes closed, sometimes moving, sometimes at rest. Defined by curved lines and over-

23

lapping forms, the figure is shown in the process of turning. Background, woman, fan and clothes are fragmented and multiplied in order to combine many aspects of a single scene in one composition. When the canvas was painted in 1913, motion pictures were becoming popular and so too were the automobile and other devices for speedier transportation. The appetite for seeing more than first meets the eye was a natural reaction to the faster pace modern life was then assuming. It was the Futurists, however, who were to exploit this idea to its fullest.

Braque's "Man with a Guitar" and Metzinger's "Woman with Fan," like so many early Cubist paintings, were more involved with physical than psychological investigations. Neither artist was concerned with his sitter as an individual but merely as a point of departure. More interested in transforming the object than interpreting the subject, they manipulated their material at will.

24. GIACOMO BALLA, Italian, 1871–1927
AUTOMOBILE DYNAMICS, 1913

Futurism, flourishing in Italy just before the First World War, was concerned with dynamic motion. As it predicted the coming conflict, it also reflected industrial developments of the period. Automobiles, trains, rotating wheels, explosive machines, frenetic dance halls—these were the spurs that needled the Futurists. Their true parents were the wonders of modern invention and the kinetic excitement of speed.

The Futurists broke up form in order to reproduce motion and, whenever possible, the complete motion of a given object at a given time. To achieve this fugitive idea on canvas or paper necessitated drastic con-

25

25. GEORGES BRAQUE, French, 1882–1963
MUSICAL FORMS, 1918, Collage

tractions, usually in the form of multiple overlapping planes. Speed tends
to fracture vision, for as we race by an object it seems to telescope into a
condensed form or even, at times, to dissolve.

In his painting "Automobile Dynamics," Giacomo Balla, father of
Italian Futurism, was less concerned with the shape of an automobile
than with its speed. By means of overlapping lines and transparent forms
he evoked the power of a highly geared machine as he also suggested its
direction through space. The Futurists, in love with modern mechanization, were militantly in favor of change, speed, dynamics and excitement.
In one of their manifestos they noted that "objects in motion multiply
and distort themselves, just as do vibrations, which indeed they are,
while passing through space."

Along with the development of Cubism came a new technique
called "collage." Combining *real* materials, such as cardboard and torn
paper, with oil paint, watercolor, charcoal or gouache, artists juggled
textures and surfaces at will. Now they depended on the most direct use
of break-up, the actual manipulation of torn or cut *tangible* materials.

Braque, in his collage "Musical Forms," combined various kinds of paper and corrugated cardboard in a strongly textured composition where variety results from *real* rather than suggested surfaces. This freedom opened up new possibilities as it broke down the conventional barriers limiting painters to homogeneous backgrounds of paper, canvas, or wood. As an outgrowth of Cubism, the technique liquidated monolithic methods.

Collage captured the imagination of an entire era. Artists began to paint pictures which resembled collage so closely that it was virtually impossible to separate the two. Though the still life by Juan Gris was executed entirely in oil, the staccato meshing of variously textured strips and rectangles fools the eye so persuasively that at first glance one mistakes it for collage, assuming that these crisp planes have actually been cut from various materials. Here is an instance where simulation rivals

26. JUAN GRIS,
Spanish, 1887–1927
STILL LIFE, 1916

26

45

reality, recalling certain "trompe-l'œil" (fool the eye) paintings of the past. In fact one could say that collage is paradoxically "trompe-l'œil" in reverse. Whereas "fool the eye" pictures simulate reality, collage does exactly the opposite, for instead of artificially evoking all manner of objects, textures, patinas and details, it depends on the real articles themselves.

Twentieth-century art has long been characterized by shorthand techniques, not surprising in an age when speed both goads and guides us. Collage with its mixture of reality and invention is typical of this tendency, for in place of carefully reproduced textures, modern artists often substitute actual materials, thus effecting an ingenious timesaving solution. Also characteristic of present-day thinking is the urge to expose working methods. In collage, contemporary artists are apt to demonstrate openly what they are doing.

But merely to combine different cut-out materials does not guarantee a work of art. Both Braque's shorthand collage and Juan Gris's longhand painting of a collage (an ironic inversion) have something in common. Each has been carefully designed in terms of cubist break-up and reconstruction. In each, multiple textured shapes combine in designs of rich variety. Different aspects of tables, musical instruments, bottles and glasses emerge to demonstrate various points of departure. Most telling, however, is the unexpected finality these fragmented forms assume when combined into well-knit organizations. As for working methods, in the real collage one is constantly aware of the artist's glue and snipping scissors. In the painting, on the contrary, one is provocatively deluded.

27. MARCEL DUCHAMP, French, 1887–1968
NUDE DESCENDING A STAIRCASE, NO. 2, 1912

This canvas, which caused an unprecedented furor when first exhibited shortly after it was painted, successfully summarizes both Cubism and Futurism. Intensifying the idea of a simultaneous experience, it shows the complete form as well as the entire movement of a figure in one composition. When asked why he thought this picture aroused such excitement, Duchamp replied, "Probably because of the shock value due to its title.... You know at that time, in 1912, it was not considered proper to call a painting anything but Landscape, Still Life, Portrait or Number such and such. I think the idea of describing the movement of a nude coming downstairs while still retaining static visual means to do this particularly

NU DESCENDANT UN ESCALIER

27

interested me. The fact that I had seen chronophotographs of fencers in action and horses galloping (what we today call stroboscopic photography) gave me the idea for the 'Nude.' It doesn't mean that I copied these photographs. And of course," he added, the motion picture with its cinematic techniques was developing then, too. The whole idea of movement, of speed, was in the air. The controversial side of the 'Nude' was not my concern. I was only involved with painting a picture.... I, myself, was most surprised at the public reaction."

In answer to the question, why he and the other Cubists were so involved with decomposing and reassembling form, Duchamp said, "In the beginning the Cubists broke up form without even knowing they were doing it. Probably the compulsion to show multiple sides of an object forced us to break the object up—or even better to project a panorama that unfolded different facets of the same object. Here the word 'gradual' is important and so is the word 'blindfolded.' It was only later we discovered that we were breaking something; it didn't make a noise when it happened."

28. JACQUES LIPCHITZ, Lithuanian, 1891–
  SEATED MAN WITH CLARINET II, 1919–1920, Stone

Jacques Lipchitz was one of several sculptors who transferred the principles of Cubism to three dimensions. Sometimes working in stone, sometimes in bronze, he simplified and reoriented the planes of his figures so that entirely new structures resulted. To be sure, the sculptor's problem differs from the painter's, especially where Cubism is concerned, for with sculpture one can walk around an object, seeing its various sides almost simultaneously, but with a painting, multiple aspects of a single form can only be evoked artificially. In his early work Lipchitz reduced the planes of a figure to an absolute minimum, retaining only the essential architectural core. Then he proceeded to disassociate these planes from their original context and reorganize them into monuments of extraordinary purity.

Though Cubism was predicated on the idea of break-up, it was nonetheless a classical movement, often acting as an antidote for the highly charged emotions of Expressionism. The best of early Cubism was marked by orderly logic, calculated reconstruction and measured rhythms. This is not to say the Cubists borrowed images from classical art but rather that they adhered to a similar impersonal discipline.

29. ALEXANDER ARCHIPENKO, Ukrainian, 1887–1964
WOMAN COMBING HER HAIR, 1915, Bronze

Alexander Archipenko, pioneer cubist sculptor, invented a three-dimensional language to turn concave and perforated surfaces into the illusion of solid form. A refined magician, he made what is seem what it is not—a widespread habit among modern artists who often prefer ambiguity to fact. It is possible that today's emphasis on break-up and abstraction grows out of an unconscious urge to escape the materialism of our age. Paul Klee once said, "The more horrible the world, the more abstract our art."

In the sculpture "Woman Combing her Hair," Archipenko opposed rounded planes to sharply concave ones, allowing light to turn negative shapes into positive three-dimensional forms. Like certain cubist painters, he inverted parts of his figure, suggesting internal as well as external masses. But more remarkable was his ability to make total voids approximate solid form. Literally breaking through a dense metal like bronze, he forced a vacuum, an actual hole, to substitute for a human head. He once said, "The form of the empty space should never be of less importance than the form of the solid mass." Modern art owes much to Archipenko. Despite his unorthodox dislocations, despite his analytic deformations, he emerges as one of the few Cubists who was able to perform relentless experiments and yet not sacrifice human or sensuous appeal. His broken figures often retain a fluid grace which sometimes engulfs them but which at best enriches them. Archipenko's discovery that surrounding space is as important as dense mass, that negative form, whether concave or perforated, can be made to seem solid, extended the boundaries of vision.

30. UMBERTO BOCCIONI, Italian, 1882–1916
UNIQUE FORMS OF CONTINUITY IN SPACE, 1913, Bronze

While Lipchitz and Archipenko were developing cubist sculpture, the Italian, Umberto Boccioni, was experimenting with three-dimensional Futurism. He wanted to do more than suggest motion; he wanted to capture it in metal. Energizing his bronze with molten activity, he gave his sculpture a vitality that recalls both natural and mechanistic forces. One feels the power of speeding winds, the drive of machine-made motors. "Sculpture," Boccioni once said, "should bring to life the object by making visible its prolongation into space." And so with a daring rarely equalled in art he "opened up" and tried to "fuse in space" his striding figure. Along with the "Nude Descending a Staircase," this sculpture set the pace for a period which was to become more involved with interrelationships than with final facts, more involved with process than with appearance. For it was not merely a speeding figure that Boccioni was after; it was the dynamic relationship of speed to the very form that speed was remaking in space.

Boccioni, one of the leaders of Italian Futurism, was both painter and sculptor. In his work, form was fractured as indeed it is when speed causes visual overlapping.

CHAPTER 5

New forms of break-up resulting from Cubism, Futurism and Collage

31. KURT SCHWITTERS, German, 1887–1948
EARLY SPRING, 1947, Collage

Relying chiefly on cast-off discarded fragments, the German artist Kurt Schwitters extended the scope and meaning of collage. For him, anything torn, unwanted, abandoned, scarred or marred, whether made of paper, cloth, cardboard, metal or wood, became inviting material from which to create a work of art. One might better say—re-create, for that is precisely what Schwitters did. He took the humblest man-made remnants and re-created them into amazingly rich, disturbingly evocative compositions. He went beyond the cubist concept of collage, emphasizing psychological surprises as well as visual ones. The Cubists limited themselves to more formal problems, to relationships resulting from juxtapositions of contrasting shapes and textures. Schwitters allowed himself greater freedom. Torn advertisements, bills, newsprint, tickets, photographs, box-covers, stamps, wrapping paper, prints, bits of cloth, wood, plaster and metal, even buttons, were all grist for his imagination. With him, collage turned into "assemblages" of infinite variety.

No one before or since has done more to take the capital "A" out of art; no one has more conclusively punctured the theory that permanent, valuable or respected materials are prerequisites for esthetic delight. With humor, irony, pathos, and with an acute sense of history, Schwitters commented on the modern world we live in. His cumulative, often dense, pieced-together compositions can be as provoking as blurred images seen from a fleeting train, as isolated words overheard on the street, as chance encounters recognized too late. Sometimes his fragmentary words, seen out of context, are merely nonsense syllables; sometimes they have associative meaning. In the collage "Early Spring,"

words like "colour and light," "exam," "carefree" may refer to spring, but obviously this is not a literal interpretation of the subject, however vividly it suggests the broken oddments that emerge after winter snows have melted. As a composition, the design has an extraordinary upward thrust which may or may not denote growth and optimism, characteristics we habitually connect with spring. To think of Schwitters as a nihilist is a mistake, for though he depended on rejected rubbish for source material, he had the vision to imbue it with new meaning and dignity.

32. GEORGES BRAQUE, French, 1882–1963
THE YELLOW CLOTH, 1935

33. BEN NICHOLSON, British, 1894–
AUGUST, 1956 (Val d'Orcia)

Georges Braque in 1935 and Ben Nicholson in 1956 each painted a characteristic large still life that recapitulated important aspects of Cubism. Though the final results differed in spirit, the two works were based on a common interest—the structural break-up of form. While the English artist Ben Nicholson belongs to that long tradition of painters who suppress personal emotions in favor of structure, Braque, equally attentive to structure, reflected his Gallic background with more sensuous textures and more tenderly gradated color. One thinks immediately of his great eighteenth-century forerunner, Jean-Baptiste Chardin. But despite surface differences, the two compositions are similar, each evolving from Cubism while yet taking liberties with the early rigid disciplines of the movement. In both cases perspective is flattened by tilted tabletops and tipped still lifes. More drastic are the deliberate distortions that condense multiple sides of objects into single views. For example, Braque breaks his bottle down the middle to include two aspects, one in shadow, the other in light. And when he squeezes a solid form into a contorted shape he is avoiding cubist transparencies while yet trying to suggest many views of the same object simultaneously. It is almost as if one were walking slowly around his still life, watching its various sides melt into a single unit. Nicholson, with different methods, superimposed curved lines over his composition, thus guiding the viewer around and behind the objects on his table. Here the shapes, while not

32

33

transparent in themselves, are given the feeling of transparency by means of a delicate linear interplay.

Though these paintings avoid psychological content, they are more than formal exercises. They are experiences, par excellence, in multiple vision and organized interrelationships. So, too, was Cubism, but break-up in both the works reproduced here takes on a new form. Now, by means of organically twisted contours, single objects assume many aspects. The focus on co-ordinated design becomes total. Every angle, curve and diagonal is played against its neighbor to forge carefully integrated compositions. Nothing is left to chance.

34. PHOTOGRAPH OF BUILDING BY **LE CORBUSIER**, DETAIL

35. PIET MONDRIAN, Dutch, 1872–1944
   BROADWAY BOOGIE WOOGIE, 1942–1943

The disorder of modern life was a constant challenge to the Dutch painter, Piet Mondrian. His total effort was directed toward order and clarity. However, in his later years he tended to subdivide his canvases into more complicated color areas. Extracting basic geometric forms from the confusion around him, he organized his material into non-objective compositions of meticulous purity. If contemporary architecture was indebted to him, he in turn depended on its severity for source material. Le Corbusier's façade, built on strong vertical and horizontal contrasts, exploited rectangular chastity with a zeal that recalls Mondrian.

Influenced by the orderly tradition of his native Holland—by its neat compact cities and spacious flat landscapes—Mondrian early turned to Cubism. Then slowly he evolved his own way of seeing, retaining from Cubism chiefly its rectangular emphasis. With misleading simplicity he now needed only straight lines and primary colors to express rigorously calculated compositions. To change the slightest relationship in one of his works was to destroy its tensions and necessitate readjustments throughout. Color, line and proportion were tightly balanced, producing the harmony Mondrian considered essential to life. Always concerned with space, he reduced his forms to a skeletal minimum.

"Broadway Boogie Woogie," a painting Mondrian made toward the end of his life after he moved to New York, reflects his delight in America. Broken into staccato color areas, the picture recalls the snapping rhythms

34

35

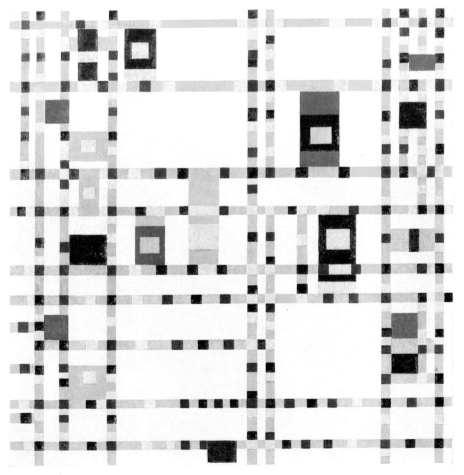

of modern jazz. The late American painter, Stuart Davis, also a jazz fan, said in speaking of Mondrian, "I talked to him about jazz several times. He responded to its basic rhythms in a direct physical way; it even made him want to dance."

36. JOHN MARIN, American, 1870–1953
REGION OF BROOKLYN BRIDGE FANTASY, 1932, Watercolor

37. HARRY CALLAHAN, American, 1912–
Photograph, 1955

John Marin's swift watercolors capture New York's animation with a stenographic speed rarely surpassed. His favorite subjects were the sea and the city, one theme embracing the restlessness of nature, the other the restlessness of man. With broken lines and tilted perspectives, Marin projects his observer into the city, making him feel its towering architecture, its rushing traffic. He borrows cubist transparencies less for structural reasons than to underline the dazzling variety of a large metropolis. By means of elision and overlapping, he crams whole urban landscapes onto one small piece of paper.

36

For American artists, Brooklyn Bridge has always spelled romance. Marin conceived of the famous landmark as a fantasy. A few brush-strokes suggest steel cables through which one sees imaginary surroundings; an isolated horse and cart, hints of moving automobiles—these are all he needed to make the bridge come alive. One bird compensates for many in a landscape where the setting sun repeats itself in high clouds. Terse, yet poetic, this broken composition covers a vast panorama despite its modest means.

Far less abbreviated but similar in feeling is a photomontage by the American photographer, Harry Callahan. A city again becomes the

central theme in a composition based on multiplication of broken elements. Steel cables and fire escapes, both familiar symbols of modern Americana, repeat themselves in lace-like profusion. Dwarfed human figures move through this maze on an infinite number of levels. Everything is fragmented, everything happens at once. It would seem that even photography owes a debt to Cubism, but in return painters have learned much from the camera. As a rule they wisely avoid competing with its literal powers of reproduction. Modern photography has done far more than free artists from the burden of realism. With its unique ability to isolate blown-up details and reveal unexpected flashes of vision, the photograph acts as a potent stimulus.

38. STUART DAVIS, American, 1894–1964
COMBINATION CONCRETE NO. 2, 1958

Another American artist to concentrate on the city was Stuart Davis. Here again is staccato break-up, so intense that at first glance this painting by him could pass for a collage. The signature, words and syncopated color all contribute to a design filled with excitement, noise and humor. Davis's use of break-up describes the interpenetration of modern city life, even to its harsh cacophonous sounds. If Mondrian appears to have organized similar material more rigidly, the American also stresses careful design while yet not sacrificing the city's strident crash and bang. One almost senses neon lights going on and off; one almost sees the reflections in garish store windows; one almost hears the dissonance of crowded streets. A realistic portrayal of the subject could never have aroused the diverse conflicting sensations that Davis was able to compress into this one semi-abstract composition. In discussing his tendency to feature invented words in his work, Davis noted, "The artist sees and feels not only shapes but words as well. We see words everywhere in modern life; we're bombarded by them." Like Schwitters (Plate 31), Davis responds to the printed word; like Mondrian (Plate 35), he reacts to jazz. "I think all my paintings," he once said, "at least in part, come from this influence, though of course I never tried to paint a jazz scene... it was the *tradition* of jazz music that affected me." According to him, another important influence stems from American cities. "It is they, I suppose, that have impressed me most. I've accepted the noise, the cacophony (to use a big word) of present-day life as subject matter. I'm a thorough urbanite—one hundred percent."

39. AMÉDÉE OZENFANT, French, 1886–1966
COMPOSITION, 1922

The French painter, Amédée Ozenfant, also reverted to conventions of Cubism in his early work, making use of transparencies wherever he needed them. In this canvas called "Composition" he took fewer liberties than usual, for most of the objects included—bottles, carafes, drinking glasses—were actually transparent. With fastidious economy Ozenfant forced each outline to perform overtime, allowing the contour of one form to define that of its neighbor. As in a jigsaw puzzle, every piece has its own place, the final composition meshing into a closely inter-locking design. Here break-up is not spontaneous; it is punctiliously controlled in order to stress oppositions; oppositions of light and dark, of flat and round, of curve and angle, of in and out, of positive and negative. Stately and impersonal, the design is built on a series of variations.

Again we find modern art depending on shorthand methods. By letting a single line record two separate boundaries, Ozenfant produced an ingenious kind of visual pun. When he wrote, "I build, I adjust, I polish my structures," he was not exaggerating. At best he produced paintings that were fabricated with the accuracy of architecture. A conscientious follower of Cubism, he took apart familiar objects only to put them together again in newly invented relationships.

40. FERNAND LÉGER, French, 1881–1955
THREE FACES, 1926

In Léger's paintings, human elements are often contrasted with geometric forms. This forthright French admirer of modern mechanization once said, "I make use of the law of contrasts which is the eternal means of producing the impression of activity, of life... I strive to build up organized oppositions of contrary values, contrasting volumes and contrasting lines." Breaking his composition into compartmentalized units, Léger here juxtaposed stylized heads with geometric surroundings. For him, the human element always remained totally impersonal. "The

human figure, the human body has no more importance than keys or bicycles," he observed. In this canvas, three profiles represent a motion picture audience, if the projector directly opposite them can be taken as a clue. Or is the reverse true? Are they instead images on a screen? In 1926 when Léger painted "Three Heads," he had been actively involved with cinema for several years, having already collaborated on the experimental film, *Ballet Mécanique*. The entire design of his painting, with its insistent emphasis on light and dark, exploits negative and positive volumes. Realizing that artificial light transforms objects, Léger played shadow and substance against each other, sometimes suggesting volume by volume's very absence.

Break-up in this canvas is twofold: first in its pure, subdivided composition; second in its emphasis on magnified details, an idea borrowed from movie close-ups. Three enlarged heads become an audience; a few rectangular shapes turn into motion-picture reels. The picture is another demonstration of how urgently modern art relies on the condensation of symbols. If Léger's composition is broken, it is also fully integrated, for he insisted on making each separate part subordinate to an overall design. Hoping that his painting would operate with the same precision as a well co-ordinated machine, he tailored every shape to this end.

41. PABLO PICASSO, Spanish, 1881–
HEAD OF A WOMAN (Dora Maar), 1943

We see Dora Maar both in profile and front view at the same time. We see her not only from two separate angles but also as she moves from one position to another. Even Picasso's curvilinear brushstrokes are adapted to the idea of rotation. At first glance, the portrait may seem cruelly distorted, but after longer observation it becomes more than a parody. Slowly one realizes that this broken face and these deliberately dislocated features are concerned with changing expressions as well as changing positions. Picasso, along with many of his colleagues, was convinced that since life is in violent flux, so also is art. Though a far cry from the formalism of early Cubism, this composition is yet closely linked to the parent movement. It is not surprising that Picasso borrowed from his own past inventions in order to develop new ones. Still interested in projecting many sides of an object at once, he now evolved a more rapid, condensed way of doing so. A few bold lines, an inverted plane or two, a frank twisting of form and feature, all add up to a startling

66

composite image. Picasso's long series of rotating figures represent more than exercises in motion; they are potent tools for strong emotional expression.

42. PABLO PICASSO, GUERNICA, 1937

43. PABLO PICASSO, GUERNICA, Detail

"Guernica," often considered the greatest painting of our century, is an apocalyptic indictment of man's inhumanity to man. The whole meaning of this canvas is centered in destruction, broken bodies and broken forms defined by a technique crude enough to suggest the savagery of war. Tortured people and frightened animals are arranged in violent disorder, their emotions revealed in one comprehensive report. Picasso has purposely included only those elements that contribute to brutality and fright, accentuating certain features, eliminating others. Sometimes he needs only a streaking head with outstretched arm, sometimes the entire helpless body. Even his jagged composition, built on disturbing contrasts of light and dark with figures rotating and transparent forms revealing each other, emphasizes mutilation. Meaning and form are so interwoven that a new visual language of fear is created.

Painted in memory of a small Spanish town wantonly destroyed by an air raid during the Spanish Civil War, this mural-like canvas summarized many kinds of break-up as it also relentlessly pinpointed the destruction of man himself. Turning back to his own earlier discoveries, Picasso forced paint to simulate the cut-out torn appearance of collage, a technique peculiarly sympathetic to the idea of breakage. He even added a painted version of shredded newsprint, not merely as a formal device borrowed from collage but also as an ominous symptom of modern communication. Again he borrowed from his past when he relied on the transparencies of Cubism to break up his figures. But here similarity ended. In place of Cubism's impersonal discipline he injected the strongest possible emotions, inventing new symbols to satisfy new needs. His tortured figures, rotating and twisting in pain, turn their wounded bodies toward a bare electric light globe (a favorite motif with Picasso). Serving doubly as symbolic sun and all-seeing eye, this feeble ray of hope illuminates a world gone mad. Painted in sombre tones of black and grey, "Guernica" grew out of innumerable studies and sketches, its angry spontaneity in no way subdued by these preliminary works.

CHAPTER 6

Break-up of content

44. GEORGE GROSZ, German, 1893–1959
METROPOLIS, 1917

During and immediately following the First World War, Dadaism (a movement named after an infant's first words) swept Europe. If Futurism foretold the war, Dadaism resulted from it. Artists in Switzerland, Germany and France, disillusioned as much by false slogans as by brutality, found relief in the negation of all accepted values. For them, willfully disorganized compilations of trash, often highlighted by shocking allusions, reflected their own nihilistic feelings. Disenchantment was the father of these men who threw traditional moral and esthetic codes to the winds. While only a few years earlier the Futurists had heralded modern life, the Dadaists now rejected it with scathing contempt, retrogressing to what seemed like infantile behavior, but what was in fact a conscious rebellion, a denial of everything they had once respected.

George Grosz, the German painter, as an early member of the movement, filled his canvases with angry denunciations of the greed, corruption and viciousness he witnessed during and immediately after the war. In a picture of 1917 called "Metropolis" he borrowed cubist transparencies to expose a forest of tottering buildings where crosses sardonically decorate blind windows. In the foreground, human dregs are on the move, without focus or regard for each other. The disorientations of man and architecture make this *non sequitur* composition an unnerving experience. Grosz smashed everything—all accepted dogmas, all traditional codes. The sanctity of religion, womanhood, love and humanity were torn to shreds. Content and form merge to express both degradation and disintegration. Later, after Grosz moved to America and to a less hostile life, his work lost much of its earlier vitriolic power.

45. GIORGIO DE CHIRICO, Italian, 1888–
EVANGELICAL STILL LIFE, 1916

46. SALVADOR DALI, Spanish, 1904–
ILLUMINED PLEASURES, 1929, Oil with pasted photoengravings

46

In 1916, when Giorgio de Chirico painted "Evangelical Still Life," he foretold Surrealism nearly a decade before that movement took shape. Thirteen years later Dali was to be directly affected by him. (Incidentally, 1929 was also the year Salvador Dali became an official member of the Surrealist group and started painting literal transcriptions of his dreams.) A canvas by Dali, called "Illumined Pleasures," shows de Chirico's influence in many ways—in its composition divided into capsule-like irrational episodes reproduced with the utmost realism, in its insistence on incongruous perspectives and shadows. Both artists included pictures within pictures as if to approximate the multiplicity of dreams. Dali added collage to his painting, using pasted photoengravings in order to accentuate the interplay of fact and fancy. By contrasting irrational content with unexpected realism, these artists made the impossible seem plausible. They virtually caused the unreal to appear "realer" than reality. Because both pictures were probably conceived in terms of associative experiences drawn from different periods in each artist's life, certain isolated episodes are less difficult to decode than the entire compositions.

73

In his early work, filled with brooding dream-like visions drawn from disconnected segments of his past, de Chirico predicted an era when Freudian psychoanalytic terms were to become daily clichés. Never to be confused with Expressionism, his proto-Surrealist paintings were not concerned with immediate emotions but rather with the newly discovered miracle of the dream and its capacity to reveal the unconscious. From this same source came Dali's paranoiac visions. In place of Expressionist exaggerations he substituted minute psychological probings. With him, obsessive images tended to replace direct emotional messages.

Though Dadaism foretold Surrealism, it was based on a totally different philosophy. While the Dadaists tried to escape disillusionment through complete negation, their followers pursued a more positive solution. For them, the world of dreams offered relief from the stagnation they found intolerable in daily life. They were convinced that dreams were the only valid reality, hence the term Surrealism or super-realism.

Dali's refined mannerisms made his imagery all the more shocking. In "Illumined Pleasures" he explored man's private obsessions with clinical accuracy. His practice of subdividing a canvas was a characteristic Surrealistic device used to duplicate the disconnected, episodic quality of dreams. Outstanding contemporary writers like James Joyce and Virginia Woolf also fractured logical time sequence with their stream-of-consciousness associations. In their work, as in Surrealist paintings, the past and present intermingle freely.

47. PAUL KLEE, Swiss, 1879–1940
EILE (Hurry), 1938, Gouache

48. POTTERY VESSEL FROM HUMBOLDT BAY, Dutch New Guinea

Paul Klee, master of the visual pun, specialist in small works of large meaning, humorist, philosopher and compassionate observer of human foibles, borrowed from many sources—from primitive art, from the immediate world around him and from humble forms in nature. The old adage that "there is nothing new under the sun" is not true. But what is new often happens to be a distillation of the past and present. Klee was a master of distillation, taking what he needed from all parts of the world, but making these borrowed images peculiarly his own. He

47

48

approached reality in the same way, fusing fact and illusion to invent a new graphic language. In his work, complexity seems deceptively simple.

Toward the end of his life, Klee stressed broken calligraphic symbols, allowing dream-like memories to guide his brush. In a gouache called "Eile" (Hurry), the title is casually incorporated in the composition, but its meaning is prophetic. The word carried a premonition of approaching death, for the first symptoms of Klee's fatal illness had already appeared, and "hurry" was a possible reminder that time was growing short. Here, the impact of primitive art is strong. (Compare the decorations on a New Guinea pot.) Longing to escape the oversophistication of contemporary life, Klee noted in his journal that "there are still the beginnings of art which one finds in ethnographic collections or at home in the nursery." He tried to uncover the wonders of nature through the innocent eyes of aborigines and children, attempting to combine their freshness of vision with his own cultivated knowledge. "I want," he wrote, "to be as though newborn... to be almost primitive." Klee's signs and symbols relate to his personal life, while the South Sea hieroglyphics result from joint experiences. In primitive societies, art is generally a group enterprise, reflecting the history of an entire tribe or clan. Today, though primitive methods are often appropriated, content is more individualistic. Thus Klee, an accomplished violinist, identified the symbols in his picture with music-like notations. Undeniably influenced by primitive art, he also understood his own century, its frailties, paradoxes and delusions, its breathtaking dimensions and awesome inventions. Yet only by innuendo do his small works reveal the complexities around us.

49. PAUL KLEE, AIR-TSU-DNI, 1927, Pen drawing

Recalling but never reproducing the lacy architecture of Tunis, this drawing, made thirteen years after Klee visited North Africa, has an enigmatic title. When spelled backward, the three hyphenated syllables turn into the Latin word *industria*, which may obliquely refer to the laborious technique used here, but more likely suggests the buzzing activity of North African native life. Klee's inventive titles are often keys to his work. At first they may seem nothing more than private jokes designed for the artist's personal pleasure, but slowly they take shape to involve larger and sometimes double meanings. In "Air-Tsu-Dni,"

76

an invented Moslem-like name is attached to a fragile composition reminiscent of textile designs. One almost senses taut threads supporting sheer fabric. Always an admirer of mellow old materials, Klee particularly enjoyed the accidents of age that transform them. He tried to approximate the irregular dimensions, the all-over patterns, the informality of ancient frayed textiles. By accepting the flat surface of his paper, precisely as weavers respect the two-dimensional limitations of their fabrics, he turned an imaginary scene into a continuing experience, projecting it beyond rectangular limits. One feels that this is only a small part of a larger city. Minarets, mosques, towers and streets all depend on intersecting, broken lines, somewhat as textile designs depend on a variety of threads. Drawing, definition and shading result entirely from linear control. Throughout, one is reminded of those secret beaded curtains that sometimes substitute for doors in the Near East. The very nervousness of each dot and dash contributes to the illusion of Oriental shimmer.

50. PAUL KLEE,
NEKROPOLIS, 1930, Gouache

Klee's visits to North Africa and Egypt undoubtedly influenced his work, but it was more likely his natural affinity for the Near East that caused these trips in the first place. Long before 1928 when he went to Egypt, the artist tended to rely on imaginary hieroglyphics as ideograph symbols. Living in an age dedicated to the printed word, he retreated from its domination by inventing his own personal signs. Typical is the gouache painting, "Nekropolis," made two years after Klee's return from Egypt. With stark symbols he summarized all the burial grounds of civilization. One recognizes not only the crypts and pyramids of Egypt and the crosses of Christianity but also the hidden tombs of innumerable anonymous men. The meticulous technique Klee used in "Air-Tsu-Dni" (Plate 49), is replaced here by broad brushstrokes better adapted to stone monuments of death. Fitting means to meaning, Klee turned technique into a tool, not an end. Through abbreviated symbols he forced his spectator to become an active participant, for it requires more than passive observation to unravel one of his small paintings.

Even before his illness, this artist was attracted by the mysteries of death. He pictured it in many guises, as hostile, compassionate, humorous and as the final liberator. Already in 1901, at the age of twenty-two, he wrote in his journal, "Then I philosophize about Death, which completes that which was not completed in life." In "Nekropolis," he not only broke up his design into symbols; he also subdivided his picture into horizontal layers, indicating the rich archaeological and cultural strata under the earth. Man-made funeral monuments rise one above the other, reminding us of historic cemeteries—of humble ones—of heroic ones—but significantly Klee leveled them all to the same dimension.

51. PAUL KLEE, DRUMMER, 1940, Gouache

52. JOAN MIRÓ, Spanish, 1893–
   DARK FIGURE AND SUN, 1948–1949

Klee, and later Miró, often depended on hieroglyphics where speed of line, immediacy of technique and fragmented symbols recalled the freedom of primitive art. Klee's "Drummer" is only an eye and two bone-like arms actively involved in the process of drumming. Miró with similar economy created a "Dark Figure" cavorting before the sun. At first glance both paintings may seem over-simple, but again shorthand methods and deliberately open designs add up to more than meets the eye. When Klee wrote, "Art does not render the visible; rather, it makes visible," he was perhaps thinking of stenographic reductions such as these where concentrated symbols describe not specific objects or scenes, but rather their ambiance. In a revolt against present-day materialism, modern art has become curiously impalpable. Figures and forms appear to lose their solidity as illusion replaces fact. The human figure, overwhelmed by abstract forces, seems bent on renouncing its identity. Artists today are concerned with processes, not with final conclusions.

In these two paintings, Klee and Miró were more interested in the act than the actor. Like the Futurists who preferred the running of the man to the man running, Klee dwelt more on the process of drumming than on the drummer, and Miró concentrated on gestures of movement rather than on the moving figure. With spontaneous calligraphy they described the spirit of an act. One feels the abandon of Miró's "Dark Figure," the ominous power of Klee's "Drummer." It was the gestures of life that these men explored. For Klee, a fragment was often more provocative than a complete object. Repeatedly his work deals with small segments of vision, with details that give promise of larger possibilities. Miró's reduced images often suggest elemental forces, a few swift lines describing suns, moons, stars, man and beasts. Both artists were probably familiar with certain primitive pictographs from the prehistoric European caves that had only recently been opened to the public.

51

53. JOAN MIRÓ, THE TILLED FIELD, 1923–1924

54. AFRICAN GOLD WEIGHTS from the Ivory Coast

Though "The Tilled Field" was painted in Paris, it was based on Miró's memories of his home at Montroig near Barcelona. The young Spaniard, having come to France three years earlier, was still nostalgic for the life he had left behind. Spotting his canvas with symbols representing a farm landscape, he divorced certain important organs from their bodies, forcing them to act as isolated instruments of communication. An enlarged ear and eye rediscover the sounds and sights of his past, while a Spanish flag flying near a French one further recalls his homeland. Droll domestic animals sprinkled throughout the composition suggest gold weights from the Ivory Coast, those small African figures that Miró probably saw for the first time in Paris where Negro art was then becoming known. Using details of human, animal and celestial bodies as clues to a larger theme, he took liberties with nature, inventing new shapes and forms to replace familiar ones.

54

55

55. SALVADOR DALI, Spanish, 1904–
PARANOIAC FACE, 1935

56. Attributed to **FRANCESCO ZUCCHI** Zucchi, Italian, c. 1570–1627
SUMMER

If this canvas by Salvador Dali is turned upright, an astonishing image takes shape to explain an otherwise obscure title. Like an Italian sixteenth century still life, which on second sight transforms itself into a monstrous human head, so too Dali's composition was intended as a double and divided experience. The frightening profile that replaces the landscape conjures up a dream in which disconnected images merge and alternate with distressing speed. Dali's act of prestidigitation was more intricate

56

than his sixteenth-century predecessor's, but the same impulse made them both propose that single facts are rarely what they seem to be, especially when taken at "face" value. Notice how signature and date are camouflaged in the earlier painting; observe how this artist disguised a human face in unexpected context.

Many modern painters have implied double meanings with single images, but here Dali does not express multiplicity with symbols performing double duty. In reverse, he turned what seemed to be oneness into plurality by exploiting two separate compositions that mutually conceal each other. The observer turns from one to the other with uncomfortable ambivalence. And that, of course, is precisely what Dali wanted. He also wanted to make what is seem what it is not, to prove that material facts are a snare and a delusion, that truth is never conclusive, that rules are belied by results. If contemporary painters have done nothing else, they have at least made us face our own ambiguous world. And the same holds true for modern literature, especially for the theatre of the absurd.

Dali, a highly eclectic painter, searched the whole history of art for images that might add fuel to his own perverse themes. Sixteenth-century Italy was only one of many sources to interest him.

57

57. MAX ERNST, German, 1891–
EUROPE AFTER THE RAIN, 1940

58. SOUTH PACIFIC CARVINGS

During the early Forties the German Surrealist, Max Ernst, painted a series of richly encrusted canvases so entangled, intricate and inventive as to defy rational analysis. Faintly recalling jungle labyrinths and overgrown Indonesian ruins, the most famous of the series was called "Europe after the Rain," a title referring to World War II. As if to predict what comes "after the deluge," this painting described imaginary destruction with exquisite finesse. Though technically unrelated to Picasso's "Guernica," it is no less an annihilating indictment of war. For here richness of surface, elegance of detail and precision of linear definition make final desolation seem even more horrifying. Erosion, disintegration and the

quiet terror of frozen death combine in a composition where one form constantly turns into another. Stalactites become aged patriarchs, debris becomes bones, shattered bodies or parts of bodies emerge from every broken rock, the rocks in turn becoming human profiles. Again the urge to charge one form with many meanings, for no single image is precisely what it purports to be. Elliptical, evasive, delusive and cumulative, this dense composition becomes a tangle of conflicting landmarks. Entrails of the earth join human entrails. Upheaval is complete, inhuman, atomic and permanent, the scene at once reminiscent of scorched deserts and arctic wastes.

Max Ernst, who long has been an admirer of South Pacific sculpture, owns several fine pieces himself. He claims that these wood carvings may have "subtly influenced" him. According to his wife, the painter Dorothea Tanning, "His work sometimes shows the same tensions, the same tendency to include intricate designs within designs and the same mysterious ascendency of white over black changing instantaneously to black over white."

58

59. IVAN LE LORRAINE ALBRIGHT, American, 1897–
TEMPTATION OF ST. ANTHONY, 1948

Once again multitudinous details slowly take form to reveal more than pulverized surfaces. Ivan Albright, American painter noted for his powers of minute observation, makes physical dissolution express moral degradation. His painting, the "Temptation of St. Anthony," with its wealth of scabrous surface eruptions, exposes the diseases of modern society. Smashed bodies, torn cloth, broken boulders are envisioned as the result of worldly sin; only preying animals are left to inherit the earth. Albright's festering surfaces contrast with the jewel-like luminosity of his technique. His scarred textures reveal life so ruthlessly as to exceed ordinary realism. In many of his paintings death is the prime motif.

Speaking of his work recently, he said, "I hope to control the observer, to make him move and think the way I want him to. For instance, in many of my paintings I'm trying to lead the observer back, sideways, up and down *into* the picture, to make him feel tossed around in every direction, to make him realize that objects are at war, that between them there is constant movement, tension and conflict. What I'm really trying to do is make a coherent statement about life that will force people to meditate a bit. I'm not trying to make a pleasant esthetic experience; I want to jar the observer into thinking—to make him uncomfortable. But I'm not telling him what to think." He added, "The reason I use an extremely minute technique is to tie down, to fuse, to crystallize various discordant elements so that my painting has a composite feeling." And so, with crumbled textures in a dispersed composition, Albright achieves unity by his very insistence on overall break-up. Once again disintegration becomes a new kind of form.

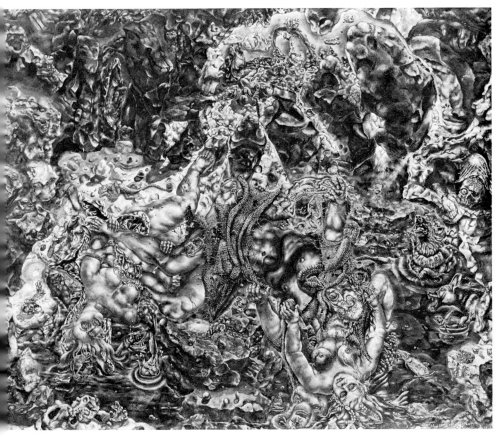

CHAPTER 7

Break-up of space

60. ROBERT DELAUNAY, French, 1885–1941
THE EIFFEL TOWER, 1909

Artists have broken up space for any number of reasons: for physical reasons in order to show various aspects of the same scene at one time, for psychological and emotional reasons, for decorative reasons. The French painter Robert Delaunay, who was closely connected with the cubist movement, painted numerous versions of the Eiffel Tower, attracted no doubt by its open structure. Using many conflicting eye levels, not unlike Callahan's photograph (Plate 37), he forced the observer to consider the building from various angles. One feels inside the tower moving up and down; one feels outside looking down and up, one even looks through the structure. This visual diversification paved the way for Cubism which, when the picture was painted in 1909, was just developing. A noticeable difference, however, kept Delaunay from fragmenting his forms as relentlessly as the orthodox Cubists did. Instead, he let disoriented space make forms appear broken.

In the past, artists tended to emphasize one direction in space, working out elaborate rules of perspective in terms of recession. They recognized that objects seem to diminish and lines to converge in the distance. But the modern painter tries to open his canvas in all directions, not alone in depth. He exploits every possibility, leading the eye up, down, back, across and diagonally into space as he adapts his composition to innumerable starting points. For those who live in present-day cities, where automobiles, elevators, subways and airplanes are all operating simultaneously in different directions on different levels at different speeds, space can become a complicated phenomenon.

61. GIORGIO DE CHIRICO, Italian, 1888–
THE JOYS AND ENIGMAS OF A STRANGE HOUR, 1913

Like a footnote from the past, the classical figure of Ariadne haunts
many of de Chirico's early paintings. Not unnaturally, this Italian artist
born in Greece turned to classical themes. In an early canvas heavy
with silence and languor, he combined a statue of Ariadne with irrele-
vant nineteenth-century architecture from Turin where he had recently
been living. The train in the background, a frequent symbol in de
Chirico's work, possibly refers to recollections of his father, who had
originally gone to Greece as an engineer for a railroad in Thessaly.
Space throughout the composition is severely distorted, each isolated
section of the canvas shown on a different eye level in different light.
Correct rules of perspective were purposely ignored in order to give the
scene a feeling of unreality, of dream-like reverie. Here, break-up of
space is a totally psychological matter. The sense of exaggerated distance,

enhanced by two tiny figures in the rear, is due in great part to irrational spatial devices. Feelings of anxiety similar to those experienced in dreams or on awakening from an anesthetic are implied; for no matter which way one turns, one never arrives. Perspective defies all the familiar rules; lines do not converge, though paradoxically figures do grow smaller in the distance, a distance impossible to identify. The composition, built on separate memories, is segmented not by line, not by pictures within a picture, but by divorced levels of space accentuated by arbitrary shadows. The source of light shifts with the same ambiguous freedom as the source of vision. Light comes from wherever the artist wishes, distance and depth also turning into man-made inventions. Scientific optical facts are forgotten in order to examine psychological mysteries. It is interesting that in later years de Chirico renounced his early work in favor of total and, alas, often banal realism.

62. **IVAN LE LORRAINE ALBRIGHT,** American, 1897–
POOR ROOM—THERE IS NO TIME, NO END, NO TODAY, NO
YESTERDAY, ONLY THE FOREVER, AND FOREVER,
AND FOREVER WITHOUT END.
(Also called The Window), 1941–1964, Detail

In a recent interview Ivan Albright explained his use of space. "As far as a model is concerned," he said, "remember that the infinite sees my model from every view-point, from every time-point, from every motion-point. The straight-on visual sight of an object is flat and if you paint with only that one viewpoint, you paint flat. One must think all around an object all the time in order to make it appear solid. That's how I happen to build such elaborate sets for my paintings. The objects, or call them models, I work with are on platforms on casters, on all kinds of movable stands so that I can change their positions, change the light on them, change their relationships at will. I don't want them to be conventional or static in any manner or form. I constantly move them around, even varying their elevations and angles. What else am I tyring to do? To compose in motion. I've learned that I can walk; I've learned that I have legs and can move and so can see objects from myriad viewpoints, from multiple angles. Look at the pot in 'The Window.' It seems to be falling; its shadows are purposely reversed. Everything in this picture has been painted from different positions, everything seems to move at different speeds, for of course some motions are faster than others. As I said before, one of the reasons I make such elaborate sets and use such authentic props is to facilitate moving my objects wherever and whenever I desire, and also to allow me to study them from all sides. With arbitrary shadows and arbitrary positions I force them to do what I want, to shock and disturb the observer. I concentrate particularly on creating compositions that are dynamic, moving, at war, in conflict. I design with different positions in space rather than merely related forms. Some objects are falling, others rising, others spiraling, others moving sideways—in a kind of controlled chaos." Space for Albright is a powerful psychological tool deliberately manipulated to control the viewer.

63. GEORGIA O'KEEFFE,
American, 1887–
AMERICAN RADIATOR
BUILDING, 1927

Artists have long painted the city. A procession of names from Canaletto and Guardi to Turner and Monet calls up the magic of Venice. Paris, too, has been a favorite subject. In recent years the metropolis, grown to staggering proportions, remains an important theme, especially for American writers and painters. Modern cities, notably at night when illuminated artificially and spearheaded by vertical skyscrapers, produce a new kind of space. Georgia O'Keeffe is only one of many American artists who have interpreted the city at night, concentrating, like most of her contemporaries, on New York. One thinks immediately of Reginald Marsh, Mark Tobey, Lee Gatch, Lyonel Feininger, Edward Hopper, Stuart Davis, John Marin. When O'Keeffe painted her version of the "American Radiator Building" at night she recognized how darkness purifies a scene as it eliminates all the details that clutter it in daylight.

With strict economy she allowed variations of artificial light to pierce her composition, suggesting the words of John Dos Passos, "Night crushes bright milk out of arc-lights..." and those of Thomas Wolfe "...everything about it seems to soar up with an aspirant gleaming magnificence to meet the stars..." "At night," said Frank Lloyd Wright, "the city not only seems alive; it is alive. But it lives only as illusion lives." This is particularly true of O'Keeffe's painting: buildings are virtually annihilated, leaving only light and space to create an illusion of perforated atmosphere where space becomes more important than form. The artist actually used light to puncture form. She also flattened distance by forcing darkness to eliminate orthodox linear perspective and by making ephemeral spots of light define a deceptively shallow depth.

The inclusion of Alfred Stieglitz' name in the composition doubtless referred to the renowned photographer's New York gallery and not to his role as Georgia O'Keeffe's husband.

64. HENRI MATISSE, French, 1869–1954
RED STUDIO, 1911

During the autumn of 1910 Matisse visited Munich specifically to see an important Islamic exhibition on view there at the time. Art of the Near East was henceforth to dominate much of this Frenchman's work. From now on the flat ornamental designs of Persian manuscript illuminations with their emphasis on flowing arabesques and seductive color never ceased to interest him. A year after his trip to Munich, Matisse painted a large interior of his studio in France, stressing an all-over pattern set against a flat monochromatic red background. Earlier, under the influence of Gauguin, Matisse had already tended to flatten his space, and now after seeing the Islamic exhibition he carried this process further, arbitrarily turning the interior of a room into a highly patterned flat design where three-dimensional form was largely suppressed and shapes were interrelated by means of disconnected but repeated color spots. Even his compositional emphasis on repeated rectangles corresponded to the design of Persian rugs and manuscript pages. But Matisse's methods were freer and far less exacting than those of the Near East, for he introduced a spontaneity rarely found in Islamic art.

It is interesting to remember that in the same year (1911) the Cubists were placing their reassembled forms in shallow space, Matisse was also

flattening his distance, but for a different reason. As the most subtle and also daring colorist of our century, he found that by respecting the flat surface of paper or canvas he could achieve greater compositional freedom. The elimination of realistic depth permitted him to play bold repetitive color patterns over the entire surface of his canvas. This room, spotted with images of Matisse's own pictures, is not burdened by naturalistic perspective, the pattern literally dancing up, down and across the painting. Having completely freed himself from realistic space, Matisse was able to design his composition precisely as he wished, and as his color dictated.

65. ALEXANDER CALDER, American, 1898–
THE BLACK CRESCENT, 1960, Mobile

The mobile, a new kind of sculpture, grows out of present-day interest in motion and space. Heretofore sculpture was static, sometimes suggesting movement but not in itself moving. Even the Futurists, enthralled as they were by speed, never became realistic enough to insist on tangible motion. Based on the idea of flexibility, mobiles are designed for action and, as they move, cut through space to present a variety of relationships. Though often operated by motors, they are not necessarily dependent on mechanization. Nature, too, plays an important role. In fact, Calder claims that nature has been his strongest stimulus. The first artist to develop the mobile, he was also the first to recognize how much the synchronization of machinery owes to humble forms in nature. For him, moving leaves, twigs, branches, clouds and birds are no less intricate and precise than the most delicate man-made machine.

A large mobile by Calder, even at rest, transforms surrounding space by the vigor of its open design. When air currents cause its various parts to move in balanced harmony, the sculpture comes alive and assumes innumerable changing patterns—now swooping, now trembling, now gliding. Though three-dimensional, mobiles are conceived more in terms of space than form. Sculptors of the past used heavier materials and were apt to plan their work for given sites, but the contemporary artist, who relies on flexible metals, designs them to cut dynamic paths through real, not simulated space. A parallel break-up is found in modern cities where space is activated by jutting buildings, changing lights, elevated billboards and moving traffic.

CHAPTER 8

Break-up of design and surface

66. WASSILY KANDINSKY, Russian, 1866–1944
BLACK LINES, 1913

The two most important forerunners of Abstract Expressionism, a movement prevalent in America and Europe during the Fifties, were Monet in his late years and Kandinsky in his early years. The latter, often considered the first artist to paint purely nonobjective compositions, discovered that emotions could be expressed without formal or recognizable symbols. Using the full vocabulary of paint and brush without relying on subject matter, he made different combinations of line, color, light, texture, motion and tone express different feelings. For the first time art was completely liberated from a given point of reference. Concentrating on improvisation, Kandinsky stressed kinetic sensations. Admitting a debt to Monet, he said, "In my youth I experienced two things which placed a stamp on my entire life and which stirred me to the bottom of my soul. They were the French Impressionist Exhibition in Moscow—particularly the 'Haystacks' by Claude Monet (Plates 1, 2) and a Wagner presentation at the Hof Theatre—'Lohengrin'." In his zeal to reproduce elusive atmospheric conditions, Monet often turned his paintings into pulsating near-abstractions. Because of his indifference to subject matter and because of his splashing color (Plate 3), his influence on Kandinsky as well as on the Abstract Expressionists was strong. In the painting "Black Lines" a sense of excitement grows out of speeding calligraphy and a centrifugal dispersement of color. The entire composition is broken into floating color shapes moving across the canvas. Already in 1913 Kandinsky had freed himself from any semblance of conventional design. Over a half century later, the most avant-garde artists in Europe and America have scarcely caught up with him. Less concerned with specific emotions than with general states of emotional intensity, he paved the way for the Abstract Expressionists who, like him, were to dissolve form, line and surface in pursuit of their own spontaneous feelings.

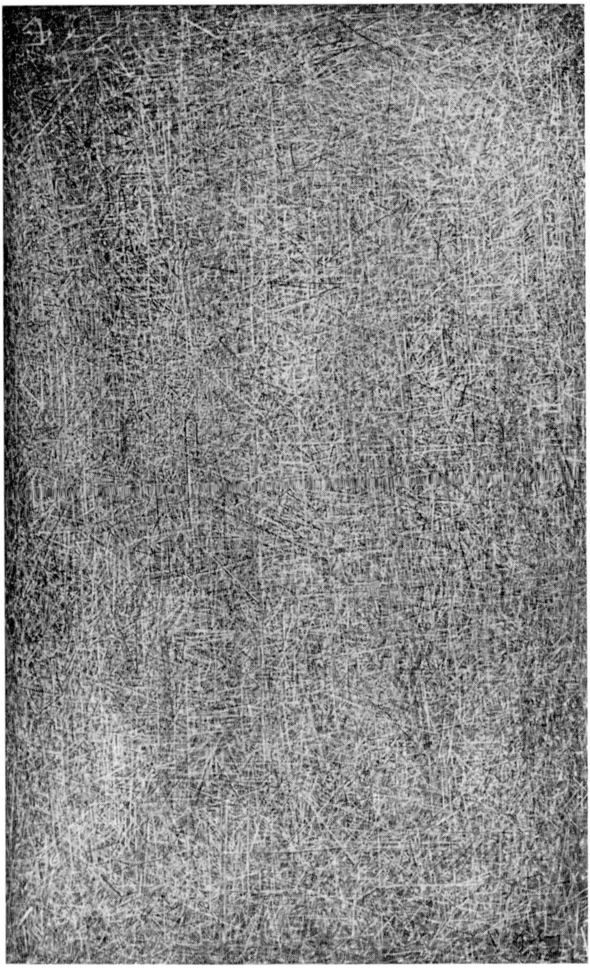

67. MARK TOBEY,
American, 1890–
NEW YORK, 1945,
Tempera

68. MARK TOBEY,
NEW YORK,
Enlarged detail

The American artist, Mark Tobey, turned his web-like surfaces into cohesive form. With a miraculous mesh of white lines he created a luminosity that gave an over-all unity to his compositions and resulted in a new technique called *white writing*. He said of his work not long ago, "In the Forties I created a sensation of mass by the interlacing of myriad independent lines. In their dynamic and in the timing I gave to the accents within the lines I attempted to create a world of finer substance. But I do not think I pursue conscious goals. The only goal I can definitely remember was in 1918 when I said to myself, 'If I don't do anything else in my painting life, I will smash form.' *White writing* appeared in my art the way flowers explode over the earth at a given time. With this method I found I could paint the frenetic rhythms of the modern city, something I couldn't even approach with Renaissance techniques. In other words, through calligraphic line I was able to catch the restless pulse of our cities today. I began working this way in England—in Devonshire in 1935—when I returned from the Orient, where I'd studied Chinese brushwork. Line became dominant instead of mass but I still attempted to interpenetrate it with a spatial existence. Writing the painting, whether in color or neutral tones, became a necessity for me. At last I had found a technical approach which enabled me to capture what specially interested me in the city—its lights—threading traffic—the river of humanity charted and flowing through and around its self-imposed limitations, not unlike chlorophyll flowing through the canals of a leaf."

No one in our century has celebrated the iridescence of modern cities more inventively than Tobey. Frank Lloyd Wright might have been describing this artist's paintings when he wrote, "Seen at night, heedless of real meaning, the monster aggregation has myriad, haphazard beauties of silhouette and streams with reflected or refracted light..."

68

69. FRANZ KLINE, American, 1910–1962
NEW YORK, 1953

70. PHOTOGRAPH OF STEEL GIRDERS

Another painting called "New York," this time by Franz Kline, is diametrically opposed to Tobey's version of the subject. Kline, also an American but almost twenty years younger than Tobey, claimed his titles were usually ambiguous. "Sometimes there are paintings that are similar, related visually more than in meaning or sources... so when my paintings look somewhat alike I give them similar titles... Often titles refer to places I've been at about the time a picture was painted..." While Kline was working on "New York" he lived near Third Avenue where the elevated railroad tracks were then being torn down. It is difficult not to relate the smashing power of this black and white open design to the kind of construction we associate with steel girders and elevated tracks. Yet only recently and shortly before his death Kline said, "I don't paint a given object—a figure or a table; I paint an organization that becomes a painting."

Instead of breaking up the entire surface of his canvas with white calligraphic lines as Tobey does, Kline reversed the process by inflating

70

a few heavy black lines to monumental proportions. However he did not merely paint black lines on a white background; the white is equally important structurally and is often superimposed over the black. Dashing on pigment with great spontaneity, he suggested the undecorated brute force we tend to identify with urban America. Our national dependence on the "loud speaker" possibly grows out of the same need for amplification. If Kline tended to negate traditional form, there is no doubt that his aggressive, jagged, open designs describe an illimitable space. His work has hypnotic immediacy; one feels projected directly into the picture, recapturing each brushstroke as it was painted. By blowing up only one structural unit, Kline was often able to describe a whole metropolis—not how it looked to him but how he felt about it as he painted.

71. PIERRE SOULAGES, French, 1919–
AUGUST 22, 1961

A painting by the French artist, Pierre Soulages, is more than nine feet long, yet does not seem unduly large. Indeed, part of its strength comes from extravagant dimensions. The picture has an enveloping power that at first glance recalls Franz Kline, perhaps because he and Soulages both specialized in predominantly black and white compositions cut by precipitous brushstrokes. But in reality there are strong differences. As a painter, Soulages was molded by his sophisticated Gallic background, while Kline on the other hand reflects America's brash force. For him, the so-called "bad taste" of this country became a nourishing stimulant. Soulages's paintings are more elegant, more polished, more discreet than Kline's and still his suspended strips of pigment have lost none of their impetuous slash. His canvases seem perpetually wet as if the palette knife had just left them. The composition reproduced here has no specific title, only a date to identify it. For both artist and viewer, meaning relies on the gratification of rich pigment deftly manipulated. In other words, the paint itself becomes at once the *raison d'être* and the image.

71

72. WILLEM DE KOONING, American, 1904–
EXCAVATION, 1950

"Excavation," with its all-over pattern and warm loam-like color, has to do with the sensations of digging into the earth, and possibly into oneself. Recalling now the swelling forms of a human body, now the flowing outlines of a Chinese landscape, the picture is filled with enigmatic anatomical curves. De Kooning claims that these symbols were not intentional and that the painting resulted from seeing a motion

picture of rice fields with people working in them. His personal feelings connected with digging up and into the earth were what interested him. He was less concerned with the process of excavating than with his own reactions to the process.

As a leader of American Abstract Expressionism, Willem de Kooning has long been involved with recording his immediate sensations experienced during the direct act of painting. Usually rejecting preliminary sketches, he allows his own urgent feelings to guide him. In the case of "Excavation," he made a richly interlocking, turbulent design with no one center of interest, no beginning, no end, no final boundaries. Though the canvas is circumscribed by its four sides, the restless composition seems to push beyond these limitations and project the artist's own reactions to a continuing experience. The painting, deliberately in flux, is not concerned with excavating but with the feelings one has while digging, throwing up the earth and delving into it from different levels. Occasionally the surface is broken by more than vigorous brushstrokes and lunging lines; it is also broken by small areas of jewel-like hues that intimate buried treasure within the earth or within ourselves. The English painter Graham Sutherland once wrote, "...the painter is a kind of blotting paper; he soaks up impressions; he is inevitably very much part of the world. He cannot, therefore, avoid soaking up the implications of the apparent chaos of twentieth-century civilization." If this is true of de Kooning, at least in "Excavation," he shows us not only chaos but hints of redemption. Instead of gesturing figures, his painting is the result of gesturing brushstrokes.

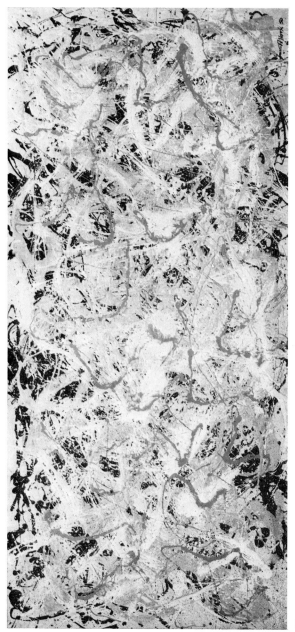

73

73. JACKSON POLLOCK, American, 1912–1956
NUMBER 27, 1950

Less disciplined than de Kooning, Jackson Pollock turned the very formlessness of his paintings into a new form. Re-creation for him was not a structural process as it was with the Cubists, but rather an intangible flow and flux where dissolution became both content and form. No one before or since has dared to ignore so completely all established rules. Pollock's paintings are the apotheosis of modern break-up. Everything is lacerated—line, light, color, form, pigment, space and texture. His dense swirling webs, drips, dribbles and tangles of paint are sometimes accused of dealing overrealistically with an anarchistic world, but the fact remains that his work was neither purely realistic nor purely accidental. It was a sensory record of his own feelings about his own surroundings, surroundings so unstable as to preclude formal definition. In America, where the emphasis on exaggeration, on youth and on too much, too fast, too soon, is part of our heritage, Pollock better than anyone expressed this conglomerate image. Obviously he did not try to solve formal problems; rather he created a new kind of fury to echo the fury within himself. Through a labyrinth of writhing pigment he offered no escape to the viewer who is everywhere assaulted by conflicting entanglements. Very different in motivation from Surrealism, Abstract Expressionism was not concerned with symbols of the unconscious, but with the artist's spontaneous feelings at the moment of painting. Abstract Expressionism and especially Jackson Pollock were the final denial of all that Renaissance and Classical art stood for.

CHAPTER 9

Break-up in sculpture resulting from new methods and materials

74. CONSTANTIN BRANCUSI, Rumanian, 1876–1957
BIRD IN SPACE, 1925, Bronze

Brancusi exploited materials to their limit, burnishing his bronze sculpture into luminous reflecting surfaces. The last great sculptor in the classical tradition, he was also responsible for important twentieth-century innovations. Modern artists, involved with new experiments in metal, owe much to his flawless reflecting surfaces where nuances of flitting light anticipated the mobile. For though his famous "Bird in Space" does not itself move, its polished surface is broken by innumerable moving reflections that produce an extraordinary sensation of speed. Technically this sculpture is not related to the disintegration often found in present-day art, its surface, on the contrary, intact and unblemished. But when reflections slither over the shining metal, form seems to decompose and movement becomes almost as tangible as in a mobile.

The "Bird," with its dancing reflections and subtle, swelling form, suggests upward motion and perhaps for that reason has sometimes been called "Bird in Flight." Clearly Brancusi was not interested in the activity of a specific bird; he was concerned with the gossamer symbol of all flight, of all buoyancy, of all freedom from earthbound gravity.

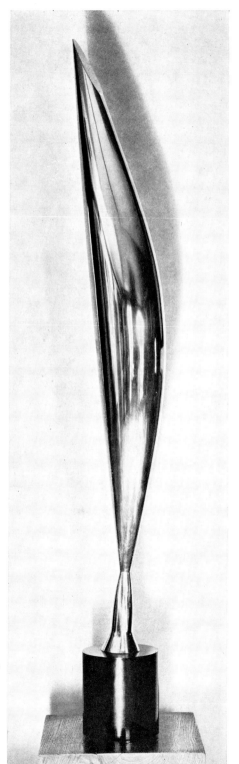

74

With him a single work habitually included more than one meaning; here he combined the idea of flight with the image of an elongated bird about to take off. The tendency in modern art to mold multiple images into a single work stems as much from Brancusi's influence as from Freud's. This sculptor's themes, usually drawn from nature, were concerned with abstracted human and animal forms reduced to their purest structures. As in his long series of birds, Brancusi repeatedly stressed anthropomorphic shapes, often phallic in feeling and always identified with the origins of life. Regarded by some critics as the greatest sculptor since Rodin, he was above all a master of condensation, forcing one telling symbol to act for the whole.

75. JULIO GONZALEZ, Spanish, 1876–1942
WOMAN WITH A MIRROR, 1936, Iron

Julio Gonzalez, generally recognized as the father of modern welded sculpture, was totally ignored during his life. Only later, when a continually increasing group of American and European artists adopted his ideas, were his works publicly honored. Starting as a metal craftsman in Spain, he later moved to Paris where during the early Thirties he collaborated with his compatriot Pablo Picasso, experimenting with him on various types of welded sculpture. A few years later Gonzalez made the iron figure, "Woman with a Mirror." Only the barest details —a wisp of hair, an open loop for a mirror, the hint of a bent arm and the curve of a woman's torso—were needed to describe his subject, but more significant than the figure itself was the way this open, irregular design became vitalized by surrounding space. The rough metal was purposely left undisguised, as were all traces of welding, a technique Gonzalez frankly adapted from modern industry. An ironic comment on mechanization, this angular figure implies that even the most seductive feminine curves must capitulate to the machine. What makes Gonzalez more convincing than his host of imitators is the authoritative power with which he invested his welded metal. Never merely decorative, his iron figures have an incisive discipline that gives meaning to each abbreviated gesture.

75

The new interest in welding completely revolutionized sculpture. Now, any open form was possible. As welding supplanted the slower processes of casting and carving, it offered a more direct, more spontaneous technique, letting the blowtorch replace chisel and fingers. Like modern painters, twentieth-century sculptors tried to bypass all established rules, preferring methods that permitted them to improvise as they worked. In a world where even children know the secrets of assembly-line production, it was inevitable that new techniques and materials would profoundly affect the artist.

76. NAUM GABO, Russian, 1890–
LINEAR CONSTRUCTION IN SPACE, 1950, Plastic and nylon thread

Using plastic and nylon threads, Naum Gabo relied on transparent materials to break through solid form. No matter where one stands, different relationships take shape as various elements appear, one behind the other. Now transparency and multiplicity are carried to the last step. Based on a mirage of complicated linear repetitions, this construction, like so much contemporary work, is more involved with penetrating space than with exploring form. The pursuit of solid form, until recently a top preoccupation in art, is no longer the dominating interest. During one of history's most materialistic periods, artists repeatedly turn their backs on materiality, trying to escape from it through the unrestricted dimensions of space. Long before "space travel" became a familiar phrase, painters and sculptors were already coping with the elusive idea. Year after year they have tried to break away from circumscribed limitations and penetrate uncharted vistas. According to Gabo, "There are literally innumerable ways of seeing my constructions. You simply can't perceive them properly from one static angle... I have done a great deal of my work in plastics for only one reason: to accentuate the transparent character of space... And don't forget that space was neglected by artists before our time. In their work they only recognized the simple fact that bodies do exist in space and that space surrounds them, whereas in my sculpture I am trying to show the penetration of space through everything—through every body, so that space becomes a part of the sculpture, a visual element equivalent to the actual material from which the sculpture is made."

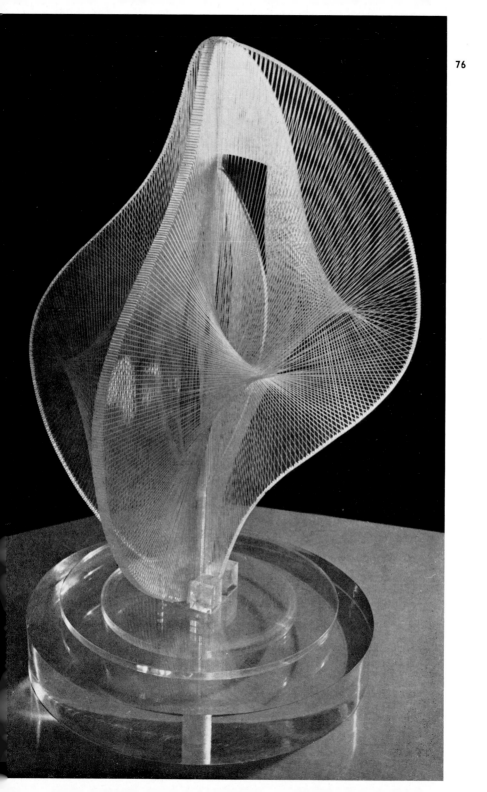

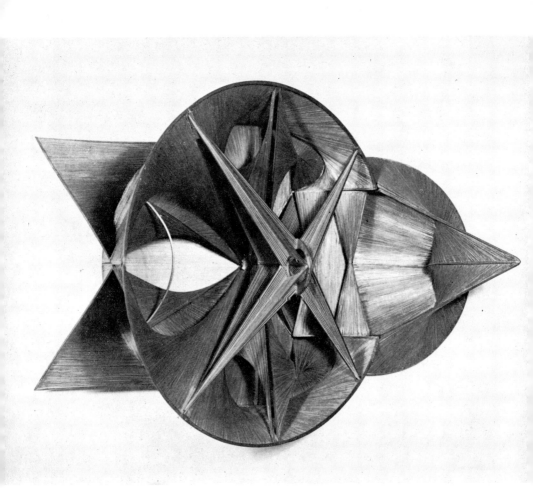

77. ANTOINE PEVSNER, Russian, 1886–1961
FAUNA OF THE OCEAN, 1944, Brass and oxidized tin

78. FUNERARY FIGURE, Bakota, French Gabon

Gabo's elder brother, Antoine Pevsner, eventually settled in France after both artists left Russia in 1922 when Soviet hostility toward abstract art was intensifying. Gabo finally came to the United States, where he still lives. The two men, who believed in "constructing" their sculpture with scientific precision, were the leaders of a movement appropriately called Constructivism. In the "Realistic Manifesto" of 1920 they stated, "We shape our work as the engineer his bridge, the mathematician his formula of a planetary orbit..." Until his death in 1961, Pevsner experimented with unorthodox metals very much as Gabo does with plastics. Breaking his forms into complex open designs, Pevsner also broke his surfaces into countless linear filaments, his work recalling certain hypnotic primitive figures from French Gabon. Negro artists of that region often preferred metal to the more customary wood, applying it ritualistically in thin repetitive strips, hoping perhaps to duplicate tribal markings with these striated designs. Pevsner stressed similar ribbed textures where rhythmic recurrence became a mesmerizing experience; yet his purpose was totally different. "Fauna of the Ocean," made of brass and oxidized tin, is designed to be looked at and into from a variety of angles. Intended to hang on the wall, the construction continually changes as the light changes and as the observer varies his

78

position. Its taut asymmetrical form and surface markings seem related to organic growth. One thinks of shells with their imprint of waves and sand; one thinks of objects shimmering beneath the water in refracted light. Pevsner's sculpture encourages light to remake its furrowed surfaces and expose its hidden hollows. The subject is not literally described, only suggested, and yet both the outer shape and inner design of this composition suggest marine life. Here Pevsner was able to adapt a pure and uncompromising technique to the interpretation of obscure undersea mysteries.

79. **ALBERTO GIACOMETTI,** Swiss, 1901–1966
TALL FIGURE, 1949, Bronze

80. **ALBERTO GIACOMETTI,** STUDY FOR TALL FIGURE, 1947, Plaster

Giacometti's inordinately tall, tightly stretched figure makes surrounding space seem vast. With all descriptive detail eliminated, it stands alone, earthbound by the weight of its heavy feet. One feels the figure has been pushed to the last extreme, that if further extended it would snap under its own rarefied tensions. The very process of paring away that produced this rigid, emaciated image is another symptom of contemporary interest in immateriality. Even the surface of Giacometti's bronze figure has been kneaded to suggest the erosions of nature. The artist reduced his means to an absolute minimum and yet repeated his favorite theme: the isolation and loneliness of man.

An earlier plaster study for the "Tall Figure" was more easily recognizable as a woman's body, the arms freer, the head larger, the form fuller. Giacometti eventually dematerialized his image, turning it into a vertical, quivering, tendon-like figure. He himself once said, "Figures were never for me compact masses but, rather, transparent constructions." Some modern sculptors have arrived at the same result by relying on transparent materials; others on open designs, but it was Giacometti alone who pierced form by reducing volumes almost to their vanishing point. No matter how poised, balanced or impersonal his figures, they always remain strangely remote as if their attenuation was caused by a great intervening distance.

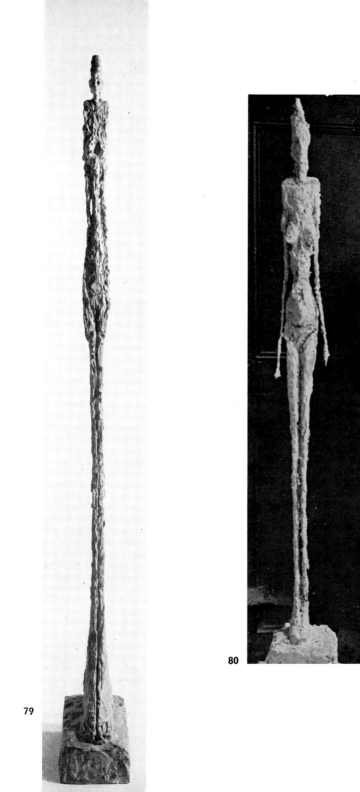

79

80

Henry Moore, who deliberately perforates his sculpture with holes in order to play light through and over it, stresses pliability. His "Reclining Figure" parallels the undulant curves of nature where rounded hills fluctuate under changing light and rocks are weathered by wind and sea. But Moore did not imitate these forms; instead he recognized their universal implications and related his sculpture to natural mutations caused by time and the elements.

Since Turner, no English artist was to interpret his own period or influence his compatriots more conclusively. Much of modern English sculpture stems from Moore's initial impact. Though in his early years he produced several completely abstract works, his approach has more often been strongly humanistic. Man is his preoccupation, but as a rule only in a wide, generic sense. Repeatedly he carves or models female figures symbolic of Mother Earth, of fertility, figures that sometimes turn into composite images where one form is suggestively contained within another. Details are minimized unless they contribute to the central theme of growth. Moore's work differs drastically from Giacometti's, for though both artists deal with man, Moore's figures have weight, permanence and grandeur. Giacometti's, on the other hand, are elusive figments of the spirit. The popular Freudian habit of identifying the feminine body with curving hills is particularly appropriate in relation to Moore's sculpture. For him, vacuums become as important as form itself. Never merely haphazard openings, they are negative forms that make solid volume seem more potent. As Moore often claims, he is breaking up space with form rather than the reverse.

82. **DAVID SMITH,** American, 1906–1965
HUDSON RIVER LANDSCAPE, 1951, Steel

"Now steel, that's a natural thing for me," David Smith once said, "I buy it in flat plates—that's the way I use it. After Cubism who cares about form? It's planes." "Hudson River Landscape," a lyrical steel sculpture welded in a continuous design, much like an unending drawing in the air, is typical of this American sculptor's indifference to accepted form. Smith made more than a hundred drawings of the Hudson River at one time when a teaching assignment took him back and forth along the river. He claimed that the sculpture was the after-image of these drawings, and by after-image he meant "dream image, subconscious image, exchange-image." The sculpture, though certainly not an obvious description of the Hudson River, does have the flow and flux, the suggestion of wave, hill and bridge that we associate with river landscapes. Smith himself once asked, "Is my sculpture the Hudson River? Or is it the travel and the vision?"

This artist was one of the first Americans to develop the technique of welding. Before he was twenty he had already become a riveter in the Studebaker plant at South Bend. His work, originally influenced by Gonzalez, is closely related to the materials he uses. One feels the tensile strength of steel, one realizes that the metal can be bent at will by means of blowtorch and heat. A more open design, a more complete break-through of solid form can scarcely be imagined.

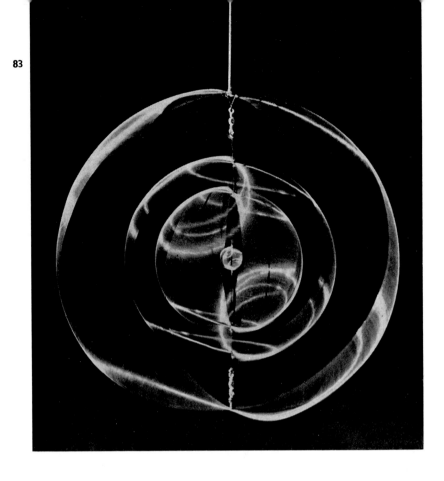

83. LEN LYE, American, 1901–
ROUND HEAD (in rotation), 1959, 4 polished rings

84. LEN LYE, ROUND HEAD (in faster rotation)

Like Calder, Len Lye also experiments with tangible motion. His metal sculpture, entirely dependent on speed, changes visually as its rate of movement increases or decreases. Usually Lye depends on only the simplest elements—flexible metal rods or, as in this case, four concentrically arranged, highly polished rings. When these are made to spin, some in clockwise and others in counterclockwise directions, they literally cut through space to produce an illusion of actual form, precisely the reverse of what one expects from rotating open sculpture. Now speed and light make form, where in reality form does not exist. Lye's constructions, usually operated by motors, are based on the idea of time. One must observe their activity over a period of time in order to understand their volatile meaning. Called Tangible Motion Sculpture because only through movement do they live, Lye's works differ from more familiar mobiles. While the latter are enhanced by motion, his sculpture has no meaning without motion. It only exists when it moves and when the original rods or rings are lost in the speed that transforms them. One view (Plate 83) shows the four rings as they start to rotate; a moment later at greater velocity they seem to turn into a solid light-struck globe (Plate 84).

The possibilities of Tangible Motion Sculpture are staggering, especially when applied to public buildings or outdoor areas. The whole perverse idea of creating form from an illusion, and of forcing speed to appear static is another extension of our present desire to make what is seem what it is not. Len Lye, working with only a few modest rods and rings, has developed sculpture that at top speed parallels the most complicated shapes in nature.

84

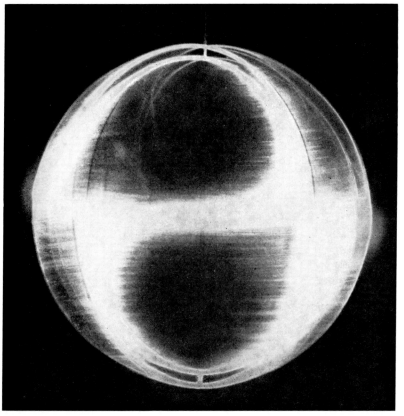

85. CLAIRE FALKENSTEIN, American, 1909–
GATES, 1961, Iron and glass

86. CLAIRE FALKENSTEIN, GATES, Enlarged detail

In Venice the American collector Peggy Guggenheim commissioned an American sculptor, Claire Falkenstein, to make a set of outdoor gates for her garden. Well over ten feet high, the gates represent a complex maze of heavy wrought iron rods in which chunks of Venetian glass are suspended by pressure. This transparent yet sturdy tangle of metal relates to the patterns in a nearby leafy trellis, both distinguished by a similar interweaving design. The glass insertions give scale to the doors as they also catch the sunlight with their reflecting surfaces. Here are gates that provide safety and privacy, yet go beyond a purely useful function. Falkenstein's twisted, knotted patterns are to be looked through as well as looked at. The visitor sees the garden in vague outline before he enters; and again, when leaving its enclosure he is prepared in advance for the outside world. The intertwining metal has an organic vitality in harmony with the leaves and vines growing on adjacent walls. A point-counterpoint composition, the design results from a variety of

86

dissident repetitions. The metal web seems at once fragile and sturdy, its delicate tracery tough enough to support heavy chunks of glass. Once more, a modern technique makes it possible to break through traditional form and, in this case, reproduce lace-like sculpture that operates successfully esthetically and functionally.

87. RICHARD STANKIEWICZ, American, 1922–
FISH LURKING, 1958, Metal

In a sculpture by Stankiewicz, break-up is not only evident but implied, for this ironic construction, suggestive of fish lurking in reeds and water, is composed entirely of broken, cast off machine parts. These discarded pieces lose their original identity as they are recombined in new context. Like Kurt Schwitters (Plate 31), Stankiewicz transforms useless, used-up relics into structures that have fresh meaning. He is most successful when his invention is sufficiently vigorous to obliterate all memory of the object's previous function. As a rule, he does not greatly alter discarded materials; it is more his method of combining them that shapes his sculpture.

Present-day artists are frequently attracted by the romance of broken down machinery. In our period, obsolescence takes over with lightning speed. The whole idea of slightly "beat-up" tarnished mechanisms is appealing. For artists today, the rubbish heap offers inexhaustible possibilities; for them the thought of rescuing cast-off machine relics only to recreate them into poetic equivalents becomes more mockery than cynicism. Contemporary sculptors are able to outwit the machine, to rebuff its infallibility. Schwitters was among the first to recognize that art does not depend on valuable materials, that the most contemptible rags can stimulate creativity as potently as the rarest alabaster. Stankiewicz belongs to a large group of artists who today are preoccupied with the same interest.

That discarded remnants can be so juxtaposed as to express valid emotions is not a new idea, but these remnants become meaningful only when used inventively enough to tell us something we have not already been told about the world around us. To do this demands a high degree of sublimation.

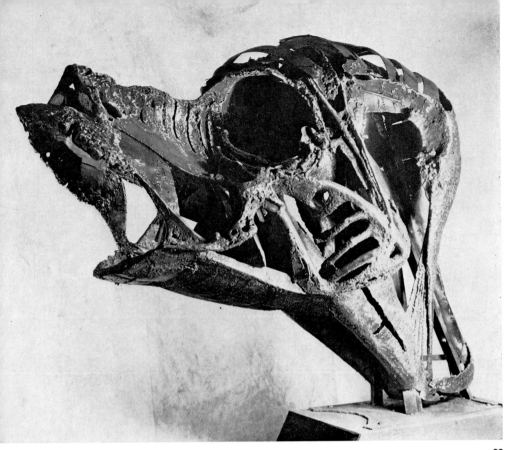

88. THEODORE ROSZAK, American, 1907–
IRON THROAT, 1959, Steel

89. CÉSAR (César Baldacchini), French, 1921–
NUDE OF SAINT-DENIS I, 1956, Iron

Perhaps the most direct break-up in modern art today is found in the
many metal figures where corroded surfaces and amputated forms
intentionally suggest destruction. Typical are a skeletal steel head by
the American sculptor, Theodore Roszak, and a headless, armless
decayed nude, made from forged and welded iron by the Frenchman,
César. Roszak's "Iron Throat" is part animal, part human, part machine,
its disintegrated form completely broken by jagged holes. It seems to
synthesize the skulls of all dead creatures caught in their last frightening

roars. Nothing remains but iron bones, for this monster symbolizes the composite violence and vitality of modern death.

César also epitomizes death but chooses an unexpectedly classical image. His nude, with its head and arms omitted, recalls Greek and Roman statues which through accidents of age have suffered decapitation or other fragmentation. But here resemblance ends, for classical sculpture relates to life and to idealized man, while César's mangled surfaces frankly deal with extinction. New techniques of welding and forging are partly responsible for both Roszak's and César's work, but no more so than new techniques of scientific destruction. These disintegrated sculptures are as close to the burned flesh of Hiroshima as certain marble carvings were to the philosophy of Greece. Many contemporary artists

89

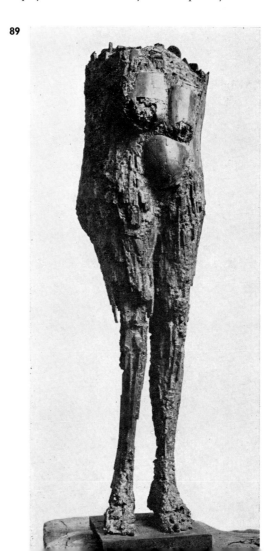

and writers argue that today's esthetics have little to do with former concepts of beauty. They find meaning in the vitality of their surroundings even when these are affected by brutality. For them to divorce art from the life around it is to deprive it of life.

90. EDUARDO PAOLOZZI, British, 1924–
HEAD, 1957, Bronze

A crinkled pieced-together metal object takes on the shape of a mangled head. Featureless, tormented and anonymous, the head is neither human

90

nor animal. It is the ultimate in desiccation. Suggesting both a battlefield and a topographical view of our own globe, this mutilated sculpture is the work of a young English artist born in Scotland of Italian parents. The piece may refer as readily to the birth of our planet as to the destruction of man, for its encrusted surface is scored by molten bubbles no less than by nail and bullet holes. It is possible that the artist intended us to accept the sculpture solely in terms of rich surface interest, but then why call it a "Head" and why insist so mercilessly on symbols of decay?

91. FRANCESCO SOMAINI, Italian, 1926–
FERITO (Wounded), 1960, Bronze

During the last few years a highly realistic emphasis on break-up has appeared in both European and American sculpture. Heretofore artists did not *reproduce* smashed-up, shattered forms; they merely suggested them. Today, however, art becomes more tangible. Take the work of a young Italian artist, Francesco Somaini. In a bronze sculpture called "Wounded" he reproduces the appearance of a large splintered rock.

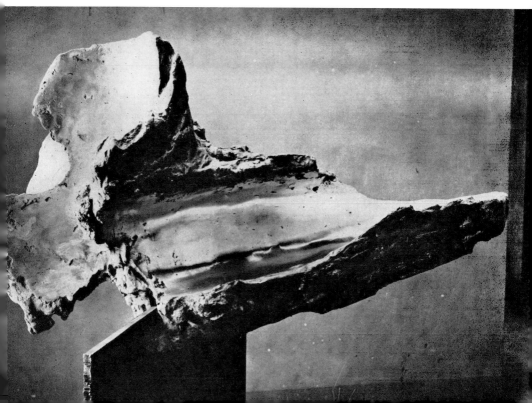

The piece has both elegance and a seemingly accidental beauty such as one might find in the natural processes of erosion. Technically Somaini is most adroit, but one questions why he conceived this work in bronze when he might have used real stone that needed only slight alterations to achieve the same results. Why create a "found object" if a real one is available? Like a pendulum, art swings back and forth. Collage is invented only to be simulated (Plates 25 and 26); so too the "found object." Accepted as an authentic form of art and often only altered by slight modification, "found objects" have become models for elaborate reproduction. The original idea that recognition and selection can invest familiar objects in nature and daily life with esthetic validity is circumvented when these objects are *produced* rather than *found*.

92. JOHN CHAMBERLAIN, American, 1927–
JACKPOT, 1961, Welded auto metal and gilt cardboard

It was inevitable that our most familiar image of crack-up—the automobile—should become source material for contemporary sculptors, notably for the young American John Chamberlain. Depending almost exclusively on the mangled metal of brightly colored automobile bodies, this artist turns bruised relics into a new kind of folklore. Paradoxically his sculpture is gay, bold and brash, its crushed and bent shapes acting as sardonic comments on the lethal dangers of modern highways. For him destruction seems less insistent than life; one feels that these broken shining parts have indomitable gusto. Authentic if also obvious bits of modern Americana, Chamberlain's welded automobile parts summarize the concept of break-up by dramatizing the results of modern speed and mechanization.

CHAPTER 10

A last word

93. PHOTOGRAPH, Shell, Detail
94. PHOTOGRAPH, Water on a Floor
95. PHOTOGRAPH, Tree Bark

Break up is only one characteristic of twentieth-century art. The urgency, however, with which modern writers, composers, sculptors and painters have smashed orthodox form is so universal as to have become the trademark of our period. But this is not a new idea, for nature in the process of growth has been breaking up matter for centuries. A shell, a few drops of water, a bit of tree bark, or any of a thousand other natural forms give evidence of how implacable is the dissolution and reconstruction of life.

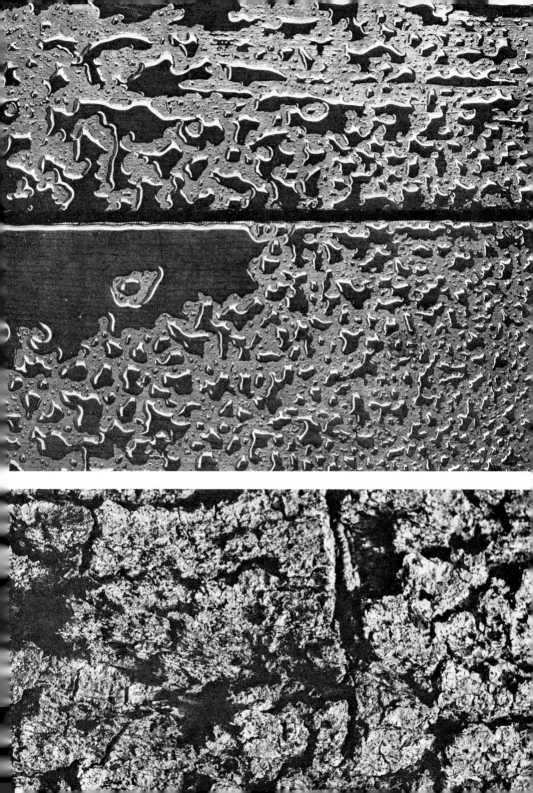

LIST OF ILLUSTRATIONS

Oil on canvas unless otherwise specified

143

145

How many books on modern art force one to try to re-experience one's own perceptions and rephrase one's own methodology? That is quite enough to put us in Mrs. Kuh's debt. Her book should prove interesting especially to those readers having already a little of the history of modern art who would like to try transforming it into a philosophy of art in relation to their own modern lives.

SATURDAY REVIEW

Artists, curators, collectors are all indebted to Katharine Kuh... Those who want to learn how to look at contemporary art will find her book "must" reading.

CHICAGO TRIBUNE

With great brevity and clarity a noted art critic conveys to the untutored or confused non-artist a sense of the motivations, meanings, and methods behind the varied aspects of "shattering" central to international modern art.

AMERICAN LIBRARY ASSOCIATION BOOKLIST